Living, Loving and Laughing

A Guide to Self-Awareness

Anthony Andrews-Speed, Ph.D.

Osmyrrah Publishing

Greensboro, North Carolina

Dedication

This book is dedicated to Cathy, Pam, Mom, and Dad,
who taught me to live, love, and laugh.

Cover Design: Lee Noel

Printed in the United States of America.

10 9 8 7 6 5 4 3 2 1

ISBN 0-9638880-0-5

Osmyrrah Publishing is a division of The Roberts Group, Post Office Box 10134, Greensboro, North Carolina, 27404.

Acknowledgments

I want to gratefully acknowledge the following persons for their contribution to the creative process this book represents.

Thanks to Dr. James N. Farr, who went above and beyond the call of duty by carefully reviewing and editing this manuscript. His contribution also can be seen in many of the concepts and models presented in the book.

A special acknowledgment and appreciation is expressed to Susan Withrow, whose careful and creative editing added an additional dimension to this book.

The following individuals, through their training or their writings, have made major contributions to the organization of my perceptions and conceptions: Dr. James N. Farr, Werner Erhard, Dusty Staub, Stewart Emery, Fritz Pearls, Alexander Lowen, Stanley Kelleman, and Ron Kurtz. And, most important of all, I thank the thousands of people who have been willing to experience, explore, and enjoy with me the never-ending processes of personal and professional growth and development.

A special thanks goes to Tom Caperton, who generously allowed his poem to be shared with those who read this book.

Finally, this book is a product of the sharing and participation of the participants in the course on which this book is based. Their courage and willingness to be themselves, and express that, allowed this book to be, and become, what it is—a testament to a group of human beings who were willing to extend themselves and to risk living, loving, and laughing.

Introduction

This book is for those of you who are willing to accept the challenge of living, loving, and laughing as if your lives depend on it. It is for those beginning or already on the path to greater self—and other—awareness. Its purpose is to create a space for you to explore—as much as you are willing—your barriers and limitations as well as your possibilities and potentials. This is your chance to become a master in and of your own life.

At present, most of you think you are limited, possibly even victimized or trapped, by circumstances and people in your life. If you believe that, you mislead yourself.

Actually, you create your own limits from your negative ground-of-being, which is the early, self-defeating decisions you made about yourself and the world from a child's point of view. As an adult, *you rarely experience your self.* Instead, you function like a robot and you achieve robot outcomes; you look to an external source for your energy, your behaviors, and your motivation. You believe you are your machinery: your mind, your body, and your emotions. But that is only what you are; it is not *who you is.* Who you is is self—a unique combination of awareness and will, in process and on purpose.

How do you discover your purpose and pursue what you want for you? How do you experience yourself alone and in relationship? How do you control your machinery and reclaim the powerful, purposeful self-in-process?

You have to go beyond your "safety net," beyond the familiar, the comfortable. You have to examine every thought, feeling, and sensation within the context of your purpose. Purpose is the self's guiding star. You need to know where you are now—what is it about your life that doesn't work—and where you are going—what do you want to create and how will you create it.

In this book, you will encounter the challenge of, and find the resources for, living your life from self, from your heart. In each chapter, you will find appropriate and practical data; applicable models and processes for living, loving, and laughing; meditations and guided fantasies for deepening contact with the self; and a few stories of other selves-in-process.

Long ago, you imprisoned your power and your freedom in a tower of old beliefs and rigid patterns. No one—a fairy godmother, a prince, this book—will rescue you. You must be your own hero or heroine.

Your contribution begins with a need to improve your life and with a willingness to participate in the process. You must decide to move from old and dead spaces within yourself to new spaces of awareness, experience, and aliveness, also within yourself.

A true master finds magic and power within. If you seek an apprenticeship with the self, for the purpose of achieving mastery in your relationships with your loved ones, your life, and the universe, this book is for you.

This book is the product of a collaborative effort between myself and the participants of a twelve-session course on mastering living, loving, and laughing. The book, like the course, contains accounts of their struggles, their barriers, and their breakthroughs. It includes some of the guided exercises that were done in the course. It provides didactic presentations of models, concepts, and processes. The most useful way to read the book is to assume the position taken by the participants in the course, which is: How can I organize this material in my own mind and behavior to maximize my ability to take the next step in my own personal/professional growth and development?

Contents

Purposes/Goals

A purpose is a creation of the self,
Becoming who it's being
Expressing where it's going to
as a function of
where it's coming from.

To get where you're going,
Know where you're coming from
And then go
from where you're coming from,
to where you're going.

A goal is an expression of the mind,
expressing who, what, when, where, and how,
specifically, observably, measurably,
the self manifests its self.

Ordinary and Extraordinary Universes

As a human being, you live simultaneously in two realms or two different universes. You live in the extraordinary universe of experience and awareness, and you live in the ordinary universe of reality and practicality. To fully experience and express the self, you must master both worlds.

You can't exclude either world. If you master only the ordinary universe, you will find success in the material world, but you also may find yourself feeling hollow; you may experience a longing, an emptiness, a desire for something more. In the other universe, you give up the material world for spiritual seclusion. You become the mystic who seems enlightened and at peace, and yet, lacks practical skills for living in the ordinary world.

This book will help you find balance. It will help you be effective in both worlds. Spiritually, you will strive for self-actualization, and practically you will learn to apply your awareness to the mundane world.

This book is a practical guide for having both worlds, for focusing your life on living, laughing, and loving. It will show you how to use *purpose* to focus on the world of your experience, and how to use *goals* to manage your ordinary reality.

Throughout the book, you will find "models" that will help you

---

MODEL 1.1 PURPOSE

PURPOSE

Internal
Be loving (start)

External
Express my love to others.

GOAL

Internal
In my mind: think "I am loving"
In my body: relax and breathe
In my feelings: access loving
    feelings

External
Give my spouse one hug per day
for six months.

BARRIERS

Internal
Fear associated with being
rejected

External
She will push me away.

STRATEGIES

Internal
Close my eyes and briefly roll
them towards the top of my head,
and then do a "body scan" and
wash out any tension in my body
using visualization and tension-
relaxation exercise. Visualize
acting in a warm and loving way.

External
Invite her out to dinner. At dinner,
share with her my desire to have a
warm, loving relationship with her
and ask her if she would be willing
to share a hug a day for 6 months
as a symbol of our willingness to
be loving with each other.

SKILLS

Internal
Relaxation Technique
Body Scan Technique
Visualization Technique

External
Give a warm, loving hug
"technique"

express what you want to accomplish. Use the models to set a general direction or to determine your intent in a specific area.

The models and mantras are tools for rewiring your machinery. Explore them, use them, become an expert at wielding these tools.

Training/conditioning vs. Awareness/enlightenment

You can operate your machinery—your mind, body, and emotions—from two positions or levels. We refer to one level as your training and conditioning. Most people function at this level; they act on preprogrammed messages, early childhood directions concerning their person-, woman-, or manhood. People who operate from their training and conditioning wander down tunnels, so to speak, in search of something.

For example, they expect to find joy and happiness at the end of a tunnel labeled "relationship." However, there's usually a grenade called "rejection" at the end of the tunnel. And every time they blindly follow the tunnel, it blows up.

The law of this level is "the best predictor of future behavior is past behavior." People who function robotically, who operate at a level of unawareness, create their psychological pain or limit their experience of life.

However, you can operate at another level, the level of awareness or enlightenment. Here, you *come from*, you *be* yourself. At the first level—training and conditioning—you are your machinery; you are your mind, body, and emotions. You identify with your machinery, and you automatically play out the programming attached to your mind, body, or emotions. This book will help you explore the path to move yourself away from your attachments, limitations, and beliefs—and toward awareness.

At the awareness level, you guide your universe. You create how you want it to be for you. At this point, you don't warm yourself by the fire; you build and light the fire. This is the level at which purpose operates.

Look at where you want to end up, and you will have found your purpose. It will be general and directional, rather than specific, observable, or measurable. It will be experiential: "How do I want to experience myself? Where do I want to come from in me—in my relationships, in my job?" Your answers to these questions define your purpose.

Purpose

Purposes are positive, but not in the sense of avoiding or denying a negative. They are positive in that they affirm how you want it to be for you, what you want to create or generate. Purposes do not deny or negate what already exists in you.

Watch how you define your purpose, because, if you state it as *not* wanting something, as not wanting to be a certain way, then you will produce the opposite effect. For example, if you choose the purpose "I don't want to get angry anymore," you inevitably will end up with anger, because that is the direction you set.

Here's how it works: Close your eyes for a minute, and *don't* see a six-foot pink rabbit. Don't see a six-foot pink rabbit drinking a martini.

Now watch how your mind handles that information. Watch how your mind struggles not to see, and yet, sees it anyway. The mind must first conjure up the image before it can repress it. So, a purpose stated negatively leads toward—rather than away from—what you seek to avoid.

A discussion about purposes

John: Can you have multiple purposes, and how do you deal with them?

Tony: You'll find that at most you have two. Exactly how many are you talking about?

John: Well, I don't know. I was thinking that learning to be more loving and learning to be more relaxed might really be the same purpose.

Tony: Because the tension that you experience, which is the opposite of being relaxed, makes it difficult to be loving?

John: Yes.

Tony: So, tension is not only a barrier to relaxation but also to you experiencing yourself as loving.

It's ironic too that while purpose is directional, it also is where you already are. Think of a purpose as something "out there," that you're moving toward. If you did not have your barriers, your training and conditioning, if you could take your patterns and negative feelings and set them aside, then you would realize that you already are where your purpose is.

For example, suppose your purpose is to be loving. Well, you *already* are loving. You were born that way; being loving is your birthright. You inherited the ability to give and receive love, to experience yourself as love. But your barriers—your beliefs, feelings, and patterns—prevent you from experiencing that about yourself.

So, purpose is where you want to head; at the same time, it also is where you already are.

Let's go further now and talk about internal and external purposes. An internal purpose defines how you want to experience you. In the case described in Purpose Model 1.1 on page 10, you want to be loving. An external purpose, on the other hand, outlines your behavior, or how you want to express your love. So, an internal purpose clarifies your intent, while an external purpose determines how you express that intent.

Goals

You use your machinery—especially your mind—to establish goals. Goals, then, are specific, observable, measurable; they answer the questions "who, what, when, where, how?" "When am I going to do it?" "What is it going to look like?" "How am I going to accomplish it?"

Be sure you align your goals with your purpose. Most people don't consider purpose; they just set up goals. Such a plan dooms relationships. In other words, you don't marry someone because you want to have 2.3 kids, a house with a white picket fence, and two cars in the garage. You have to commit, not to a structure or form, but to a process. If you commit to a form, then when that form changes, your commitment disappears. So, make sure your goals spring from your purpose.

How to Set a Goal

◆ **Eliminate traps.** You can sabotage your goal in a number of ways. Remember, your mind will divert you from your purpose because it believes it is captain of the ship. And the more loopholes present in your goals, the more opportunities you give your mind to distract you from your purpose. So, if you leave it open-ended—like "Every time I disagree with someone, I'm going to tell them"—you risk failing. If you confront everyone you disagree with, your life will be chaotic.

◆ **Define what your goal looks like to you and accept that your perception of the goal may be different from someone else's.** For example, the goal is to be more loving. What does it mean to be more loving—specifically, observably, measurably? Being more loving to Carol may mean she will give a warm fuzzy to her boyfriend every Monday, Wednesday, and Friday at 7:35 P.M. While to John, being more loving may include taking his wife to dinner on the third Thursday of each month. In other words, it will mean different things to different people. We define love as giving the other person space to be the way they are, as well as the way they are not. Also, loving requires a willingness to tell the other person where you are and where you aren't. So, if you want to accept our definition, how would you phrase a goal?

A discussion of goals

Tony: All right. Will someone give me a purpose and a related goal?

Ann: To be more loving.

Tony: Okay, can you create a goal for that purpose?

Ann: Well, I've written down 'have no expectations of others.'

Tony: That goal contains some traps. First of all, you stated your goal negatively. Second, it's not specific enough. And third, you're bound to fail, because, unless I've read you wrong, I don't think you will never have another expectation of anyone. Do you? So, reword your goal: make it positive; make it specific; make it realistic.

◆ **Be specific.** The more general your goals are, the more likely you will not achieve them, especially if you use universal qualifiers. Omit words like "from now on," "every time," "always," "never." Allow yourself space to be off purpose occasionally.

Being Pulled Off Purpose

Look at those situations that pull you off course. Look at the person in your life you avoid sharing your feelings with, the person you tend to agree with even when you disagree. You want to stand up and be loving with them, which means you tell them when you disagree, as well as when you agree.

For example, let's say you notice that you withhold or close down during staff meetings at work. Whenever you're in a meeting and the boss grimaces at you while he asks, "Does anybody disagree?" you choke. Well, that's when you want to focus on your goal.

Your purpose, in this case, is to be honest with people. What is your goal? You might say, "When my boss looks at me in the next staff meeting on Tuesday morning and asks if anyone disagrees, I'll raise my hand and say I disagree (if I do, of course)."

Identify and anticipate times when you encounter your barriers— fear, anger, hurt. Be ready when your mind tells you to withdraw or defend. You need your purpose and your goal, a specific goal, so you won't drop back into your trap.

Reprogramming Yourself with Mantras

A mantra is a personal affirmation about yourself that supports you as you encounter the barriers of your training and conditioning. It enables you to come from yourself, to stay clear about your purpose.

When you use a mantra, you are replacing or overriding one thought process or program with another. You are using your mind to devise an alternative response or behavior rather than to figure out why you resort to old patterns.

Trying to figure out why you continue a certain behavior is pointless and endless. It doesn't matter. The idea is to notice every time you experience yourself on automatic, and then use your mantra to slow down the preprogrammed response. Eventually, the old response will disappear.

The thing that perpetuates the preprogrammed response is your attention, your attachment to it. You believe it, and even worse, you act it out by doing absurd things. The man who grows impatient waiting for a train to pass might race the train across the track, honk his horn, or pull out his 357 magnum. Your belief reinforces the pattern, makes it stronger. And then, the pattern generalizes, spreads like a ripple in a pond. So, eventually, you respond automatically, not just when a train gets in your way, but when anyone or anything gets in your way.

Control Through Mastery

So, you have to be willing to use some control—not petty control in which you resist and deny what is already inside you—but a type of control I call *mastery*. Control through mastery occurs within the context of love and compassion. You acknowledge your craziness, all your training and conditioning. If you resist that part of you, you remain stuck in it, because whatever you resist in you persists.

Let me tell you about my experience of control versus mastery. My favorite participation sport is white water anything: rafting, canoeing, kayaking. I just like white water. I was kayaking down some white water

---

About mantras

Tom: While driving over here tonight, I had to stop for a train; I was already late. And I remembered my dad would rage if he had to wait for a train. But, I think because I had written down my purpose earlier, I turned off the radio, sat back, relaxed, and watched the train go by—which is unusual for me. I just decided that it really didn't matter.

Tony: That's exactly the process I want you to do "out there," so that when you find yourself in situations which propel you into your training and conditioning, you instead shift into focus on your mantra. If you can't find something better to do with your mind at that time, say your mantra. That's the time to use it; it's also the time you will least want to use it. So, make it precise. Have it ready, and make it easy to use.

---

in the mountains recently, when I rolled over. I experienced the water directly, and it was powerful. Instinctively, I responded, "I'm going to control this," and so I did *all the things they tell you not to do.* I attempted to set up to roll the kayak upright on the standard, right hand side, but the flow of the water was such that drawing the paddle in the prescribed manner to right the kayak didn't. My fear was that I would be trapped in the upside down kayak under water, so I fought/resisted the water's force by attempting to stick my head up beside the kayak above the water. Again, the water said no.

The water became my teacher then. The water was big enough and powerful enough to let me know that I would go where it wanted me to go. So, I decided to give up control, to give up my resistance, and "go with the flow," literally. Instead of fighting against the forceful flow of the current, I angled my body and paddled to catch the force of the current, which pushed me and the kayak upright. I went where the water wanted me to go, and made that the same place I wanted to go, by getting off my position and including the water's "purpose" in my purpose. A powerful lesson!

When I accepted my position, when I allowed external forces to operate, I expanded my sense of ownership responsibility and mastery. Changing my focus, my need to control, allowed me to move to another level, to the level called mastery. I discovered that, by a very small movement of my body, I could gently redirect my body without resisting forces I couldn't control; I worked with the force instead of against it.

Allow whatever is there to be there. Use you mantra to master, not to control, your programming. Don't place your mantra up against your craziness. Go ahead and let the craziness be there. Let it go and then focus your awareness on the mantra, while synchronizing your breathing. Don't struggle with your thoughts, because you will lose.

Off Purpose

What pulls you off purpose? Like magnets, your training and conditioning pull you off course. You begin on purpose—"Boy, I'm going to be so loving"—and then back in the relationship, you interact with your partner or coworker; they say something that triggers you, and suddenly, you find yourself off purpose again.

You know when you are off course through a universal alarm system which includes what Stewart Emery calls *yellow alerts*. The yellow alert is a signal from the universe; it's feedback, usually from other people, that tells you you've gone astray. Typically, we perceive a yellow alert as an attack. To maintain the old position, we deny it or we defend against it through aggression or withdrawal. We respond inappropriately and take it personally. We pretend the other person's comments determine who we are. Actually, nothing anyone says is ever personal; it has nothing to do with us. It is an expression of where *they* are.

Thank You For Sharing

Let's look at the difference between a defense against imagined criticism and acceptance of feedback. If I say to Mary, "That outfit you are wearing looks terrible," what would you expect her reaction to be?

It could be defensive: "Who asked for you opinion?"

About controlling goals

Tim: Should a goal always be something you alone can control or does it require interaction with someone or something else? For example, if my purpose is to get a job, which goal would be better for accomplishing my purpose: "I will do the following four things in order to try to find a new job" or "I'll find a new job by September 1?"

Tony: Probably the former goal would be better. And to make it more specific, you could plan to set up at least two interviews a week until you find a job. You could expand it further to include exactly what you would say in those interviews. Make your goal realistic and controllable.

Sarah: So you're better off having a goal that doesn't depend on anyone else?

Tony: Yes. Make sure you can accomplish your goal, that you can control it. Be specific, linear, practical: Here's where I am and here's where I'm heading. My purpose then gives me the general direction, and my goal provides a milestone; my goal tells me when I'm off purpose.

Or it could be acceptance: "Thank you for sharing your opinion."

It seems senseless for Mary to feel hostile and hurt by comments by someone who probably doesn't know what he is talking about. There's no need for her to take my comments personally.

How you interpret what someone says or does to you indicates where you are. Your reaction to what people say or do depends on your self-image or self-esteem. If you have a low self-image, you base your responses to self and others on your internal tapes—your beliefs and your judgments about the way the world is.

You don't have to respond in a hostile way to criticism—either imagined or real. You can respond with a *koan* and remain on purpose. A koan can move you to another position. The koan, "Thank you for sharing," acknowledges the feedback. It's not an evaluation or judgment, but an alternative to hooking into or taking personally someone's comments or actions.

You know the only thing you have in life, at each moment of life, is your experience. Reacting defensively robs you of your experience and obstructs your purpose.

Actually, you don't have to defend; you don't have to do anything. Just let it be. If you have some thoughts or feelings you've resisted in the past, then let them be. Be bigger than they are. Doing nothing about the comments or the feelings allows you to continue on purpose.

Is a koan, like "Thank you for sharing," useful in communicating with someone who understands its intent? Yes. The koan forces you out of your programs, your taping, and into your experience. When you say, "I appreciate the feedback; thank you for sharing it," you experience the feedback on a new level, the level of awareness.

In the past, you probably took it personally and hooked into a game. So, even if you overuse the phrase, it still accomplishes its mission. The koan breaks through habitual thoughts about, and responses to, barriers. It assists you in staying on purpose.

Yellow Alerts

A yellow alert, such as a hostile reaction to a comment, is a signal that you've gone awry. And when you encounter a yellow alert, don't defend by attacking or withdrawing. Use it for what it is: feedback.

Feedback is not right or wrong, good or bad; it is a statement about where the other person is. Use the feedback to come from awareness and to adjust your course, to make a correction.

If your partner gives you feedback, such as "I love you and care about you; I want to create our relationship so that I experience how much I love you," then your partner's on purpose—if your purpose is around love. But, if your partner says, "I think I've fallen out of love with you," then your partner is giving you a yellow alert. At that point, you need to say, "Wait a minute. We need to make a correction. Let's talk about it."

When you receive a yellow alert, make an adjustment. You'll have many yellow alerts on your way to your purpose. Stay conscious, centered, and do what's necessary to stay on purpose.

Going through barriers, handling the yellow alerts, may upset and threaten you. You will be tempted to defend and revert to your negative ground-of-being; your mind will incite you to protect, instead of correct.

Protection, however, is appropriate when a relationship becomes chronically painful or dangerous. That is a red alert! At that stage, you say, "I'll meet you at the lawyer's office, or in divorce court; it's just too much." You take care of yourself, and you consider the relationship a lesson to grow from.

Most people, however, protect when they should correct. They defend and protect themselves, which guarantees the outcome they try to avoid. When they protect and deny, the pressure builds until, finally, it buries them. When you hold onto your resentments, your hurts, you shrink your relationships to a level of "I'm right, and you're wrong." You might justify the end of the relationship by claiming you fell out of love, but that's a lie. You buried your love; you lost touch with it, and it feels as if it's not there.

In the yellow alert stage, you make adjustments—constantly. Stewart Emery compares it to flying to Hawaii. After liftoff, the plane shifts to automatic pilot. Automatic pilot can do two things: detect when you are off course as well as make the necessary adjustment.

Let's look at a relationship on automatic pilot. Let's say John detects when the relationship veers off course and Mary makes the correction.

In "flight," John informs Mary that they've picked up a head wind, and Mary responds, "I'll make the adjustment, so we stay on course." Later, John says, "We've picked up a tail wind; we need to drop speed," to which Mary says, "Okay, I'll correct." Again, John says, "Now, we've picked up a side wind." By this time, Mary who has been making all the adjustments, gets fed up and says, "Why can't you leave me alone? Stop telling me what to do." And the plane, the relationship, plummets to the ground.

Actually, an automatic pilot impartially corrects based on feedback it receives. People, on the other hand, take personally the need to correct.

You can correct your thinking, your behavior, your feelings. You make an internal correction. For example, Larry's wife may give him the following feedback: "Larry, I experience you as being cold, remote, and unloving in our relationship." Instead of saying, "How could you say something like that? Remember the roses I bought you on Valentine's Day?" Larry could say "Hey, I'm going to be centered about this." He contacts his awareness and meditates on the feedback. And while reflecting about the feedback, he realizes that, in fact, it may be true. He's been depressed, which has led him to withdraw. So, in adjusting and correcting, he considers how he can manage himself so he's more in touch with how he wants to feel and be in the relationship.

Let's get back to your flight to Hawaii. Although you spend 95 percent of the trip off course, you touch down within five minutes of your estimated time of arrival. So really, you've been on course, on purpose, all along.

Protecting or defending against feedback can be dangerous. If you don't correct, you may end up in divorce court instead of enjoying the island breezes with the one you care about.

Strategies

The last two steps of the Purpose Model include strategies and skills—what I call S & S—the paths to your purpose.

You need a strategy to reach your purpose. Don't expect to return to a relationship in which you've been cold and distant for ten years, and suddenly be loving and expect the same from your partner. You need a strategy. How will you implement your goals; how will you make them happen?

Strategy is your map.

Consider Larry's problem again. Larry needs an internal strategy so that he can experience himself as a loving person. Look within yourself for an internal strategy. Here's how:

◆ Close your eyes, rolling them towards the top of your head. (The action facilitates access to the altered state of being centered.)

◆ Conduct a body scan: start with your feet and move up through your body to the top of your head. Wash away body tension through visualization or relaxation exercises.

◆ Create guided fantasies, or pictures depicting how you want to be, and then see yourself being what you fantasize.

Guided Fantasy

There are a number of ways you can do the guided fantasy exercises that begin here and occur in successive chapters. One way is to read the guided fantasy exercise aloud on to a cassette and then play the cassette back with your eyes closed in an open, comfortable position. Another way would be to have a friend read the guided fantasy to you. Find a way to do the guided fantasy exercises and, enjoy.

Let's do a process now called a guided fantasy. Through this process, you will access the place within you we call your center, your safe space. From there, you will investigate your purpose and select a mantra which will support that purpose. Begin by either lying down or sitting up. Get as comfortable as possible and assume an open position—arms and legs uncrossed. Fine.

Close your eyes now. Take a couple of deep, full breaths. Really stretch your belly and your lungs as you do so. Exhale and collapse. Take another deep breath, filling, expanding, and then exhale, permitting yourself to let go, to relax. Fine.

Use your body now to trigger deeper relaxation. Focus on the trigger point between your eyes. You can relax the frown muscles between your eyes in two ways. You can tighten your eyes, squeeze them as you would against bright sunlight. Really feel the tension as you squeeze tighter, tighter, tighter. Then inhale, and imagine oxygen flowing into that area, absorbing the tension. Finally, relax your eyes, and exhale through the mouth. Fine.

Or you can roll your eyes up and "look through" the top of your head. Feel the tension, the tightness, and hold the position for a moment. Then take another deep breath, and relax, let go; breathe easily, comfortably, effortlessly.

You also can focus on the jaw area—your jaw, lips, and tongue—to initiate total relaxation. Let your lips, teeth, and jaw relax enough so that your breath flows easily through your mouth. Notice that a wave of relaxation flows from your eyes, to your jaw, throat, neck, chest, and stomach on down to your hips, thighs, and calves. Imagine any tension and discomfort flowing out through your toes, like water out of a spigot. Any remaining tension flows down your shoulders, to your arms, hands, and out through your fingertips. Relax, be at ease, breathing comfortably as you do so.

Now, do a body scan starting with your feet. Rate the feeling or energy level of each area of your body—your feet, calves, thighs, and so forth—on a scale of minus 10 to plus 10. Minus 10 describes extreme pain. Zero indicates a lack of feeling, a numbness; and plus 10 defines comfort, relaxation, a positive tingling. Move up through each area of your body, taking your time. As you scan, allow any feelings to surface and flow out of you; let them be. Stay with the scan until you feel totally relaxed, and enjoy being in your body.

Relax your mind now. Imagine walking down a hallway toward an elevator. If you don't "see" any pictures, that's okay. Try to hear the sound of your footsteps and any other sounds in the hallway. If you don't see any images or hear any sounds, that's okay, too. Try to feel what it's like to move through space to the elevator. When you feel yourself standing in front of the elevator, look to your right and press the button on the panel. The elevator door slides open. Step inside now and turn around. See the door slide shut.

Now, look above the door and notice the brightly colored number 20; notice the shape of the number 20. Then look off to your right and notice the numbers 1 through 20 on the panel. Press the number 1 and watch above the elevator door. Focus your eyes on the numbers as they change, on the colors of the numbers as they change. As I count from twenty to nineteen to eighteen to seventeen to sixteen to fifteen, let go easily, comfortably, relaxing to fourteen. Thirteen, twelve, eleven, ten, nine, seeing the colors and then the numbers changing to eight. Seven, six, five, four, three, two, one. Go down as low as you will allow yourself to go. That's fine.

Let the elevator door open now and imagine stepping out into a safe space, a special place of yours where you can go to be yourself, a space where you feel comfortable, secure, at ease. You don't have to pretend or cover up, or struggle here. The place may be a favorite childhood haunt. It may be real or imagined. Create it vividly, using all your senses. What do you see in this place? What do you hear? And most importantly, how does it feel? Can you create feelings of comfort and acceptance here?

Step further into the space now and find a spot to sit down. Settle down now. It's okay for you to just be here, with no expectations, no demands. Enjoy yourself for a moment. Now imagine off to your left in your safe space is a door. Stand up now and walk to the door. Reach out and open the door.

When you open the door, see yourself as a child. There you are as a child, standing there looking at you. Look down at this child and see

---

Finding a mantra

Sarah: I don't think I found a mantra. My child had a lot to say about how bad things were for her. So I just listened and tried to find out what she expected, what caused her to feel confused, and what created her indecision.

Tony: Actually, I wanted you to go beyond the negative feelings to the time *before* she was confused, before she was indecisive. But that's all right. For now, take as a mantra, 'I am clear,' inhale; 'I understand,' exhale.

Kathy: Tony, my child said she had to do what everybody said to do, that she felt powerless and sad. So my mantra became, 'I am important; I am powerful.' Is that okay?

Tony: That's it, yes.

---

the child looking up at you. Notice how you feel as you see the child looking up at you. Be aware of your feelings as you see the child.

Reach out and take the child's hand. Embrace the child, yourself as a child. Thank the child for coming, and then lead him or her by the hand over to where you sat earlier. Sit down now, face to face, with the child and ask the child what threatens it, what scares it, and listen.

Then find out what the child does to protect itself. What did you learn to do—long ago—to make it, to survive in the world? Find out from the child what price it paid. Listen to the child speak from the heart, from your heart. Allow the child to finish the sentence: "What I had to do to survive, to protect myself when I was hurt or afraid or threatened was . . ." Listen to what he or she decided to deny or cut off, to not feel. Be aware that the child's decision came, not from the heart, but from the need to survive.

Now ask the child to share with you the way he or she really is. For a moment imagine that you are that child and share with the other person the way you really are. And listen carefully and hear yourself saying, "The way I really am . . ." Behind, underneath the hurt and fear, let the child tell you the way he or she really is: "The way I really experience me is . . . or the way I really am is . . ."

And let the completed sentence be your mantra. I want you to find two words to add to the sentence fragment "I am . . ." These words describe how you want to experience yourself, how you really are. The completed sentence is your mantra; it will be your purpose. Stay with the child until you have two words, adjectives that describe how you want to experience you through the heart of that child. And then, thank the child for coming, for being there, and for sharing with you. Lead the child back to the door and say good-bye.

In using the two words in meditation, think/feel/sense the first word while inhaling, and think/sense/feel the second word while exhaling. Synchronize thinking/feeling/sensing the words with your breathing.

And now, imagine that you are meditating, still relaxed and breathing deeply. Inhale, "I am . . ." Exhale, "I am . . ." Assume now that some other thought or feeling intrudes, tries to pull you away from the meditation. I want you to allow the other thought or feeling to be there, and *focus on the meditation.* Stay with your mantra. Fine.

Now, see yourself in some place, in some situation you will be in within the next week or two, and know that the meditation will help you stay centered. Imagine yourself in that situation, meditating, using your mantra, whenever the situation tempts you away from your center. See, hear, feel yourself focusing on the meditation, using the mantra as a tool so you don't hook into and play out old behavior patterns.

Good. And now, out of that space of peace, relaxation, and calm, out of that meditative space, when you are ready, open your eyes.

To make the guided fantasy more effective for you, personalize the process. Some people, for example, don't like elevators; they can take the escalator. If you would rather go up than down in an elevator, go up. Some people "see" clearly as they meditate; they visualize. Others focus on sounds; they hear things. Still others focus on feelings; they intuit their surroundings. Whatever works for you, personalize and customize the meditation. Notice what works best in moving you from ordinary consciousness to that altered space.

Using Your Mantra To Stay on Purpose

Here is a sample of a purpose and mantra.

Purpose: To be more loving and to feel loved.

Mantra: "I am loved, and I am loving." Inhale—"I am loved." Exhale—"I am loving."

For some of you, the process of finding a mantra will confirm a purpose you have already chosen. For others, the process will allow you to discover your purpose. Take twenty minutes to focus on your mantra, especially when you can relax and be calm. Eventually, you'll use your mantra when you need it, to keep you centered, to keep you from jumping into a game, or abusing yourself or someone else.

The effect of using your mantra daily is cumulative; the words acquire an energy of their own and impart that energy to you. Now, if you want to test your mantra in a stressful situation, go ahead, but only if you can give yourself permission to fail. Usually, you have to build up some

26

power before you can effectively use your mantra in situations in which your mind resorts to training and conditioning.

Be careful that you don't use the mantra as another wall. Create a situation in which it's appropriate to use the mantra because the mantra will help you focus your mind or stay centered. Don't make the mantra another barrier.

For example, if your mantra involves being powerful, you don't want to use the mantra in such a way that you feel powerless or controlled by your mantra.

You will run into barriers as you work with your mantra. Your mind will make you feel powerless and inadequate. So stay with your purpose.

Using your mantra

Anne: You know, it seems easy in here. But when I think about using my mantra out there, I feel scared.

Tony: Close your eyes for a second and go back into the meditation and contact the child. Tell the child what you fear

Anne: I'm afraid I won't be able to control you.

Tony: Keep your eyes closed; keep your eyes on her as you tell her that. What do you see her doing?

Anne: I see her not listening to me; I see her rebelling.

Tony: And can you recall an experience in which she lost control?

Anne: Yes.

Tony: Tell her what really hurts.

Anne: It hurts because I want people to pay attention to me, to love me, but I don't know how to do that. And I get frustrated and lose control; I nag and demand, and then they don't want to be around me.

Tony: And if you go ahead and reach out, if you go ahead and love anyhow, you're afraid that . . .

Anne: I'm afraid that I'll be rejected again, that I'll fall back into feeling hurt and angry.

Tony: The only way through the fear, specifically the fear of rejection, is to go ahead and love anyway. If you decide to love anyway, you experience the fear until it disappears. And then, you are free to experience what is left—which is the love.

And reinforce and clarify it by completing the worksheets. (See Purpose Worksheet 1.2 below.)

Everything you do flows from your purpose. Each moment, ask and answer the question "Am I on purpose?" Then, you can begin the return trip to your original self, to the way you already is.

WORKSHEET 1.2 PURPOSE

PURPOSES
Internal
The way I want to experience me/you/it is:_______________________

____

____

External
What I want to achieve is: _______________________________________

____

____

____

GOALS
Internal
In my mind, I want to think (specific thoughts):__________________

____

In my body, I want to sense (specific sensations): ________________

____

In my emotions, I want to feel (specific feelings): ________________

____

External
What I want to do is (specific behavior):_________________________

____

____

WORKSHEET 1.2 PURPOSE

BARRIERS
Internal
In my mind, the thoughts that interfere with/stop me from thinking what I want to think are: _______________________________________

____

____

In my body, the sensations that interfere with/stop me from sensing what I want to sense are: _______________________________________

____

____

In my emotions, the feelings that interfere with/stop me from feeling what I want to feel are: _______________________________________

____

____

Happiness

Happiness
is a function of
Being
Where you is
When you is
What you is
Who you is

Mind Games: You Don't Have to Play Them

Guided Fantasy

*T*his fantasy helps you explore your barriers to using meditation as a *tool for centering, as a way to focus your energy on your mantra instead of on your game.*

Get comfortable now and relax. Begin to stretch your lungs. Inhale and then exhale; let it out, relax. Take another deep breath, inhaling, filling, stretching, expanding. Then exhale, giving yourself permission to let go, to breathe easily and comfortably.

Now do a body scan starting with your feet. Rate each area of your body on a scale from minus 10 to plus 10. At minus 10, you feel so tense, so uncomfortable that you experience pain; at zero, you feel numb; at plus 10, your body feels warm, comfortable, pleasurable.

So, start your body scan at your feet, moving to your ankles, then to your calves, and so on. Move up through your body at your own pace. As you scan your body, notice areas where you collect tension, where you hold. As you relax, notice if any areas feel particularly tense, uncomfortable, or numb.

Focus on those areas of your body that feel tense. Imagine inhaling a cool, blue, relaxing wave that flows into that area of your body and absorbs the tension. When you exhale, imagine breathing out the tension. Inhale and fill the area with that cool, blue wave. Exhale the tension or discomfort. Repeat until you feel relaxed.

If any areas of your body remain tense, focus your awareness on that area. Don't concentrate on it—just shine your awareness on it; simply be present with the tense area. Put the tension on the scale from minus 10 to plus 10. Imagine the tension assumes a shape or form; then imagine that it acquires a color. Focus on it and be aware of it. Breathe into it and notice if you can move your experience of the tension up or down the scale. Fine, now let that go.

Now take a moment to review the last few weeks of your life and notice what you did or did not do in relation to being on purpose. Did you meditate and focus on your mantra? Are you using it in your daily life? Notice if you did or didn't do the meditation over the last few weeks. If you did a meditation, under what circumstances did you do it? Did it work for you?

Now, consider if, over the last few weeks, there were times when you could have done the meditation but didn't. Remember the times you allowed yourself to assume old patterns, games, and traps. Notice when you functioned automatically. What did you use to get out of that trap? Did it work? Just reflect back over the last few weeks; be aware of any images, feelings, or thoughts. Just become aware of what worked for you and what didn't work for you in terms of the meditation and the mantra.

All right. Now just take a moment to ask yourself, "What do I have to ask, say, or do today to be on purpose?" When you have answered that question to your satisfaction, open your eyes.

When to use meditation and your mantra

John: I had a big presentation due last week and I had to wait outside the board room until they were ready for me. At first, I was tight and nervous. So, I began to meditate as I waited, and slowly I started to relax. And then I focused on my mantra. By the time they were ready for me, I was relaxed and confident. The presentation went well, and I felt good about it.

Tony: Great. That's the perfect time to try out meditation and your mantra.

More about when to use meditation and your mantra

Anne: I have trouble finding time to do the meditation during the week. I feel that I have too many responsibilities and commitments that must be met first. So instead of meditating, I find myself doing all those other things I feel I need to do.

Tony: Okay, through the guided fantasy, you noticed how often you meditated, if and when you didn't, as well as how you justified not doing it. "I didn't have enough time"; "The situation wasn't right"; "I had too many other responsibilities." You became aware of the barriers that your mind used to avoid doing something good for yourself.

Did you notice the outcome of your avoidance? The outcome of the rationalization is game. Whenever you argue with yourself, you end up in your negative ground-of-being, which in your case, Anne, leads to confusion, indecisiveness. So, Anne, when you're confused, how does that feel?

Anne: I feel stuck, caught in the middle, wanting to do two things at once, which of course I can't do.

Tony: Close your eyes for a minute. Take a moment to recreate that indecisive space, where you are confused, where you feel pushed and pulled, without direction. Pick any topic you want, and say out loud whatever thoughts come to mind.

Anne: Well, I could go to the workshop on Monday night, but I don't think I want to because it's too much trouble; I'd rather stay here. But then again, I really need to know more about myself. But it costs so much. Still, I need to do some personal work. Really though, I'd rather spend the money to go to the movies. And anyway, I need to be home more with the kids, spend more time with my mother, and cook a decent meal for my husband.

Tony: Okay, keep your eyes closed, and do a quick body scan; notice any tense areas. Take a moment to check out your feelings. After generating all those confused thoughts, how do you end up feeling?

Anne: (Sighs) I feel awful. I feel helpless or trapped.

Tony: What was the sigh about? Why did you sigh?

Anne: Because I suddenly felt afraid, and then I felt sad.

Tony: Okay, open your eyes. Do you see how your confusion and indecisiveness lead you into sadness and fear?

Game vs. Mantra

Mind games actually lead you to the feelings you seek to avoid: fear, sadness, or anger. When you act on what your mind tells you, you lose sight of your purpose; your destination then becomes confusion. Remember, your mind is a product of your training and conditioning; it is not you, the self. So when you use only your mind (your training and conditioning) to handle your life, you drop out of self and purpose and into game and ego.

Whenever you feel trapped, use the meditation and mantra to evade the games and to move on through your barriers. The meditation overrides the confusion you create in your mind and enables you to alter your path or pattern. Together, the meditation and the mantra distract your mind from the games it plays.

The Strength of the Meditation Habit

Ideally, you should meditate daily, whether you think you need to or not. Through daily meditation, you develop a habit strength so that when you encounter situations that ordinarily would lead to game, you can move more easily and quickly into your mantra, your purpose, your self. After all, loving, living, and laughing are functions of the self, not of the mind.

As you can see, your mind is your greatest barrier. It blocks your experience of your aware self and thus, of the extraordinary universe. Remember that you can approach life from two places: the ordinary universe and the extraordinary universe. (See Model 2.1.)

We spend most of our time in the ordinary universe where we base our daily lives on our training and conditioning. We live out of ego, which is the mind operating out of its tapes, programs, and patterns. Living becomes linear, and many times, automatic.

But, we can choose to live from another universe—the extraordinary universe. It is extraordinary, because the experience of it transcends daily life. At this level, amazing things can happen; in fact, miracles can occur. In the extraordinary universe, you can directly experience the self, because this is the realm of the self.

MODEL 2.1 UNIVERSE

EXTRAORDINARY UNIVERSE	ORDINARY UNIVERSE
Self	Training & conditioning
No time	Mind (Ego)
Nothing	Negative ground-of-being
Eternity	Daily life
Awareness	Time
Experiencing	Falling in love
Living	Games
Here & now	Imperfection
Being in love	Form
Creation	Emotion
Loving	Body
Laughing	Thoughts/words
Purpose	Tapes
Mantra	
Perfection	
Miracles	
Truth	

Be in Love vs. Fall in Love

In the extraordinary universe, you know love, not as a form—as being married, having children, buying a new house—but as a direct experience. Here you *be* in love, whereas in the ordinary universe, you *fall* in love. In the extraordinary universe, you experience love because you create it, because you create yourself as loving.

In the extraordinary universe, you find awareness, experience, and loving, in the ever-present—not just the here and now, the past, or the future. There is no time here, only eternity. Your purpose, your goals, and your mantra spring from the extraordinary universe, as well. And of course, you find loving and laughing here, too. Living, loving, and laughing are a function of the self, an expression of yourself, of who you is.

Negative Outcomes

So how do you know whether you are operating out of the extraordinary universe (out of your self), or out of the ordinary universe (out of your training and conditioning)? Use your outcome as a signal. What outcomes do you end up with in your daily life?

When you find yourself in your usual game, with the usual bad feelings such as fear, anger, and indecisiveness, you operate from the ordinary universe. Whenever you find yourself in your negative ground-of-being, in your soap opera or melodrama, know you are in the ordinary universe.

What is negative ground-of-being? Your games lead you to a negative payoff. In the ordinary universe, you set it up so that you and everyone else are imperfect. Use the bad feelings as red flags to alert you to game-playing. And remember that in the extraordinary universe, you and the rest of the world get to be perfect.

Keeping One Foot in Each Universe

Actually, mastery requires that you have one foot in each universe. You need to move easily from one to the other. Most people are so familiar with the ordinary universe that they forget about, or are unaware of the extraordinary universe. And so, they exclude the possibility of miracles in their lives. Miracles are a direct experience of the extraordinary—the direct experience of the self. It is here that you immediately and directly discover that you are more than you think you are.

You don't want to give up control in either area. Keep one foot in each universe. Be in both worlds simultaneously. If you can originate your actions in the extraordinary universe before moving into the ordinary universe, then you will be a master.

Mastery of Living, Loving, and Laughing

Living, loving, laughing. Mastery of each depends on your being in touch with your own experience. Living involves your experience of using your mind, body, and emotions. Loving is you experiencing yourself and others from the extraordinary universe, and being willing to express that in your relationships. And when you are willing to live and love, then laughter follows. You get the punch line of the cosmic joke. You can laugh at yourself, not derisively, but in the sense that you allow your self to be; you don't wallow in the soap opera of the ordinary universe. At the same time, you don't avoid what you need to do or experience; you go on, with joy and a sense of humor.

What is Reality—the Ordinary or Extraordinary?

Typically, we believe that the ordinary universe is real. But actually, it is illusion. The extraordinary universe, on the other hand, is real, because that's where center, or being centered, exists. Still, we have a body, mind, and emotions in the ordinary universe; and we have to deal with those, but from a distance, from the extraordinary universe. We stop believing we are our mind, body, and emotions, and know we are simply self.

We are amazingly attached to our ordinary side and we resist leaving it. We spend a lot of time on the daily stuff of life, on our survival and security needs. We invest our energy in putting it all together—who we relate to, where we work, what we eat, where we live.

And even when we've satisfied those needs, we recycle them. Even when we have our ordinary lives set up, we start playing a new game—the "more, better, different" game. We drop into our negative ground-of-being—we feel insecure, inadequate, hurt—and then we tinker with the system in order to feel better. We continually manipulate the mechanics because we're unaware of the other universe.

Handling the Mechanics

What we forget or fail to realize is that once we have handled the mechanics, we are free to move on and explore other domains. We can fulfill our potential; we can become self-actualized. But we stay locked in, focused on aspects of the ordinary universe, instead of taking the next step, of moving into the extraordinary realm.

There will always be jerks out there; there will always be games; there will always be the mechanics for you to handle. You may decide that a relationship is toxic, in which case you begin another process called looking for a new job or filing for a divorce. Still, those actions occur within the ordinary universe. How do you get to the other side?

You have to generate that yourself. You have to create how you want to be, where you want to come from. For example, you know other people love you, not by what they give you or say to you, but by your willingness to create yourself as being loved.

The Universe Within

We believe the universe is ordinary because the mechanics jolt us into ego, into survival and defense. The dailiness captures us and takes control of our awareness so that we forget there is more. And then life becomes a process of getting by, getting over, getting through it all without much love or joy or happiness.

There is a whole universe inside of you. From within, you can create how you want to be. You can come from your negative ground, from your pain and suffering, or you can come from your capacity to love, to

---

Applying the extraordinary realm to work

Joan: I have trouble seeing how you can apply the extraordinary realm to working, to a job. I mean, I just don't like my job. Of course, I realize that my dislike is a function of the ordinary universe.

Tony: Yes, it is. First, step back from work, from you at work, and look at where get stuck in your job. Is it the work itself? Is it the atmosphere? Is it the boss?

Joan: Well, it's mainly the boss. He's an S.O.B.

Tony: Okay. He's probably not the first one you've ever met, is he? So, you might as well learn to deal with him. It's okay to think he's an S.O.B. Focus on your approach to solving the problem of working with him. From the ordinary universe, you would deal with him from fear, anger, control, defense. In other words, you use your boss to justify dropping into your negative ground-of-being, which allows you to have the negative payoff of hating your job.

From the extraordinary universe, you can choose to look at your boss and your job as a learning experience. You may need to learn how to deal with this type of person so that you stay on purpose. Ask yourself: "Where do I want to come from when I'm dealing with my boss, when I'm dealing with any problem?"

---

create, to enjoy—to be perfect. Do you see the contrast between what you are—your mind, body, emotions—with who you is—your self, your essence, your awareness? Model 2.2 illustrates the aware self and the mind as it operates vis-a-vis the self.

MODEL 2.2

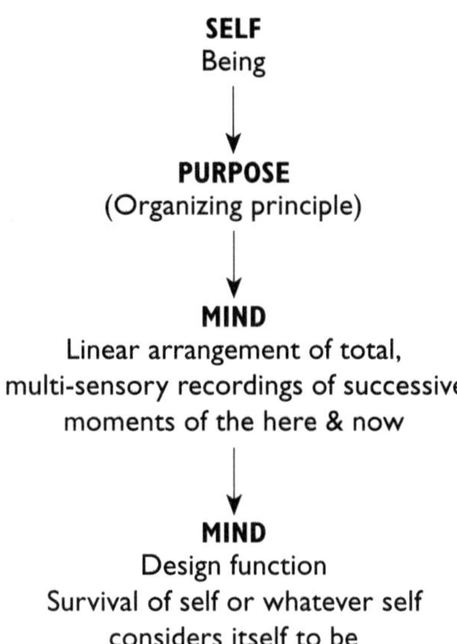

What is Self?

What is being or self? In the beginning, you be. You, as a being, appeared in the extraordinary universe. And, out of your self, you created a purpose, an organizing principle for living.

Now, as you came into being, you acquired a mind. Assuming we all have a mind, what is it? What's your definition of the mind? Is it a biological computer? A tape recorder? Actually, it's both.

Werner Erhard defined the mind as a "linear arrangement of total, multi-sensory recordings of successive moments of here and now." That means that as we live, we experience. We generate experiences. All the experiences we generate become our lives. So from birth (or maybe even before) until we die, our minds make total, multi-sensory recordings of each moment of our lives. When we have an experience, our minds record it and then file each recorded experience in a linear arrangement in an internal bin or filing cabinet.

The contents of the file cabinet are only representations, however; they are not the truth about our experiences. Let's say you have a memory of sitting at the kitchen table when you were five years old. And you remember that your mother was baking you a birthday cake. Now what really happened and how do we know it happened?

Experience vs. Recording

Actually, we don't know what happened exactly because we don't have sufficient data. All we know for certain is that you had an experience of being five years old. Actually, your memory could have been a hallucination brought on by the anesthesia you had for an operation when you were nine years old. We just don't know.

All you can know is what you *experienced* happened, which may or may not be what *actually* happened. Our experience of life through our minds can only be illusory. We believe we are what we call ourselves—males, Americans, mothers, lovers, and so on. And we have a set of concepts around what it means to be each of those things, to perform those roles. But most of us are living out of prerecorded fantasies that are disconnected from reality. When we live out of those fantasies or illusions, we are living *out of our minds.*

Your mind is a fantasy machine, a fantasy-creating machine. You need to stay unattached from the mind's fantasies, because your attachments keep you in the ordinary universe. It is your mind that creates the arbitrary values, meanings, and concerns in your daily life. When we become attached to the mind's truth, then we confuse fantasy with the real thing, with the experience. At a minimum, believing the mind's fantasies leads you to limiting yourself and your life; at a maximum, your attachment leads to pain and suffering.

So, you can be attached to the mind or you can live from the self, from being, from purpose. Even then, when you come from the extraordinary universe, you will still experience the highs and lows. There will always be lows. But, you create a system for dealing with the lows so you are left with the highs. Then, you experience a continually expanding sense of joy or love, which comes out of the extraordinary universe.

So, check it out; examine your experience. Where is it coming from? Is your experience coming from the mind, from your negative ground-of-being? Or is your experience coming from your purpose?

The Mind's Original Purpose: Survival of the Self

Actually, the mind has a purpose of sorts. Its purpose is survival. But, survival of what? The mind's original purpose is the survival of your self, your essence, your awareness. It promotes the continuation of the self or of whatever the self considers itself to be. So, the mind supports your aliveness and awareness as long as it operates for survival of the self.

Through training and conditioning, our culture teaches that you are not here to be alive and aware, to experience joy; instead, it teaches that you exist to promote and follow the culture's mores, your parents' beliefs—all of which later become your tapes. After training and conditioning, then, the survival of the mind becomes the survival of your tapes or your ego. (See Model 2.3.)

MODEL 2.3

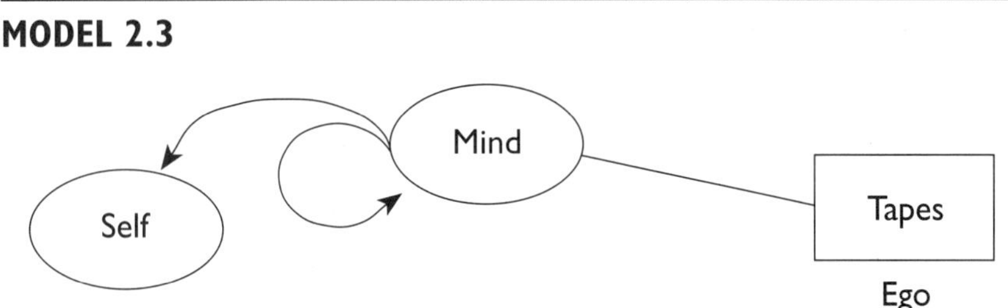

The Mind's Distorted Purpose: Survival of Your Tapes

So, the mind, that perfect and powerful machine that once operated for the survival of your self, turns on you. It begins to operate for the survival of your tapes, your beliefs, your positions. Of course, some of your tapes are necessary and useful; we're concerned about the destructive tapes, the ones that keep you from being alive and aware, the beliefs that you're inadequate and imperfect.

The mind doesn't have a purpose, because purpose is a function of the self. And the self is not the mind. The mind's design function is its own survival.

The mind doesn't distinguish between positive and negative, good and bad. It is a machine, automatic, linear. It simply records and stores away your experiences, all of them. How you apply those recordings later on determines their value.

For example, let's say Joan meets Tom. Joan notices that Tom's wearing a tie. At the same time, she unconsciously remembers that her father wore a tie, too. Then, she gets a little closer to Tom and she notices his hair is graying; her dad had grayish hair, too. And then, she scrutinizes Tom's face, and do you know that he has the same expression on his face that Dad did? Joan hated her father, and she decides she doesn't particularly like Tom either. So, what is she doing?

She is accessing an old tape, an old recording she made of her father. The recording of her father includes the data that Dad is a man; he wears ties; he has grayish hair; and he wore a certain expression on his face. Because of the recording, she filters her impression of Tom. She generalizes her experience of men based on the recording of her father and ends up interacting, not with Tom, but with Dad.

The Mind's Need to Be Right

That's how the mind works. Because its design function is survival, the mind will fight to make certain that it is right, and that you, as self, and everyone else are wrong. Being "right" indicates your mental position, which originates in your tapes. If I can show that your mental position, your belief is wrong, then that makes my belief right according to the mind's design function.

Now being right doesn't always imply the assumption of a one-up or best position. It also can mean that you take a position of one-down, or least. Either way, your position comes out of your mind, or your tapes and beliefs. (Model 2.4)

MODEL 2.4

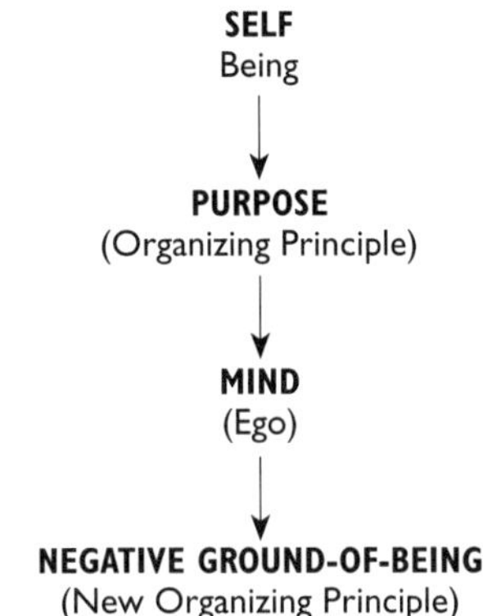

After a time, these one-up or one-down tapes acquire a life of their own. They no longer just sit on the shelf of your biocomputer. They begin to invade your life, your being, until the recording becomes everything you're thinking, feeling, sensing, and intuiting. The recording becomes your experience.

For example, imagine that early in life you have a direct experience of a round red. Your mind records it, and places it in a linear arrangement in your file cabinet. For now you file away your experience of a round red. But later in life, you encounter a square red. Or do you? You experience the square red as a round red.

We don't live in our experience; we live in our tapes, in our recordings. And we use our tapes to play "if only": If only Dad had loved me, then I could be loving with you now. If only Mom hadn't been so hostile and rejecting, I could be more trusting now. Whenever the mind confronts a situation which threatens its survival, whenever it perceives threat, it reactivates the old tapes in the filing cabinet. In fact, the mind's need to survive is so strong, that it will actually kill the body in order to make sure its tapes survive.

How do you reach the point where you believe you need to commit suicide? You have to justify it. The attempted suicide that comes into my office rarely admits the act was illogical. Typically, he recites the reasons he should kill himself: "My wife left me; and I got busted for child abuse, and then, I lost my job, and then . . . " His mind creates justifications for doing something crazy, unaware, and alien to the self.

The mind lacks awareness. It is a powerful machine, and when it justifies old beliefs or runs old tapes, it's difficult for us, with our training and conditioning, to resist. We believe it and start acting it out. We live out of our filing cabinet, rather than out of our experience.

So, what makes the contents of the file cabinet so seductive? What does the file cabinet contain? Three groups of filings or categories seduce us into believing the mind: first, second, and third degree upsets.

First-Degree Upsets

In a first-degree upset, you experience physical pain and a perceived threat to survival on a relatively unconscious level. Some examples include getting burned, sustaining injuries due to a car accident, broken bones, bee stings.

Second-Degree Upsets

A second-degree upset is a perceived loss with unexperienced emotion. When I say unexperienced emotion, I mean that the emotion stays stuck because you never handle it. For example, let's say you have a traumatic, threatening experience which stirs up some fear and some anger. And instead of experiencing those feelings, you hold them in and push them down. You go to your father's funeral and act wooden and stoic. You refuse to feel and give expression to the sadness, the grief, the anger. Other examples of second-degree upsets are divorce, birth of a sibling, loss of a parent.

Third-Degree Upsets

The third-degree upset simply reminds you of a first- or second-degree upset. Watching a death scene on TV or in a movie that triggers your memory of a parent's death is a third-degree upset. Or perhaps you are in a new relationship and your new partner acts like someone you had a disappointing relationship with before and you think, "Oh boy, here it goes again."

The guided fantasies and personal work you have been doing act as reminders of third-degree upsets. When you bring up the upset, you can look at your tapes, and how you use those tapes to play your games. You then can experience out the upset, instead of replaying it compulsively, which frees you from it.

Birth As the Original Upset

What is it like prior to birth? It's comfortable, like an air-conditioned apartment. You experience the love of self and the love of your landlady. But, eventually, you are evicted from this Garden of Eden, and in a very disturbing way. You are pushed, pulled, shoved down a narrow tunnel. When you finally emerge, you encounter cold air, bright lights, and physical abuse. And then, you look around and see your landlady who looks pretty bad. Before you can get your bearings, your are carted off to a room full of screaming beings. You are isolated, alone, in shock. So what are the various elements of this multi-sensory recording?

You experience physical sensations such as being squeezed, pressured, along with feeling cold, and maybe even pain. Sometimes you choke; you can't get your breath. And the lights are so bright, they hurt your eyes.

During the first year of life, what percentage of time do you think the infant spends in a first-, second-, or third-degree upset? How much time does it defend against being in those states? The infant probably spends about thirty percent of its life in a state of upset. And that's a conservative estimate.

What happens in the second year of life? The percentage of time spent defending against upsets is substantial, and cumulative, year after year. By age five, according to Freud, the child's decisions about himself and the world are pretty well set. From then on, you have few direct experiences. You spend most of the rest of your life defending against or filtering your experiences through your mind's distortion of the truth.

What can break you out of these preset patterns? How can you break out of your negative ground? How can you move over into the extraordinary universe?

Will Coupled with Awareness

Research suggests that people with cancer must cope with an overload of second-degree upsets, or perceived losses. If they handled it by dropping into their negative ground-of-being which said life was not worth living, they suppressed their own immune systems, which made them vulnerable to cancer.

It is possible to move into the extraordinary universe through the self rather than through the mind. In the beginning, you had yourself, your being. Out of your self you created a purpose, which we now call your mantra, around which you organized your life. Then you acquired your mind, which originally assisted you in survival of the self and its purpose. (See Model 2.2 on page 39.)

Things changed when you adopted your training and then operated against, rather than for, you. You began to pretend you were your mind, and your organizing principle for life became your negative ground-of-being. (See Model 2.4 on page 43.)

Still, your mind can work for you when you remember it is a machine. Later in life, a significant emotional experience or awareness can rattle the sediment. Imagine your personality as sand at the bottom of clear water. What happens when you put a stick into the water and stir the sand? Eventually, the dirt settles down, but its structure has changed. Likewise, a significant emotional experience can alter your patterns.

So, look for your unexperienced experiences. Notice how you sabotage yourself, how you limit and hurt yourself. And then consider how you really want to be. What do you want the organizing principle of your life to be? Do you want to organize around your negative ground-of-being, around pain and suffering, or do you want to reorganize it around your mantra, around love, around being happy? It's up to you, not as mind but as self.

Awareness

There is no you. There is only me.
You are a representation of me.
By understanding me, I understand you.
By loving me, I love you.
By serving me, I serve you.

Defense Mechanisms: Can't Live With Them; Can't Live Without Them?

Guided Fantasy

Close your eyes now, and breathe deeply. Take a few moments to center yourself as you move into a meditative space. When you are ready, allow a scene to form in your mind. Bring the scene in from the left. See yourself as a teenager. Then see your parents, one or both, criticizing and attacking you. Hear what they said. And then, focus on your reaction to their words. How did you feel? What did you think? Fine. And then notice what you did, as a teenager, to protect yourself from the words. Notice your mind's reaction. Did it wipe it out, distort it, exaggerate it? As a teenager, how did your mind handle that perceived threat? Now, let that scene go off to the right.

Bring up another scene. This time, see yourself as a child, being severely criticized and attacked. Picture yourself receiving a message from someone else, a message that you're not okay in some way. Hear what was said, and look into the mind of that child, your self as a child. Notice what that child believed about itself, decided about the person giving the message. How did that child react, deny, defend, protect?

How did that child's mind protect itself from those upsetting feelings, from that threat? Play the scene out, and when you've noticed how the child's mind reacted, let the scene go off to the right.

Now, bring in another scene from the left. This scene includes your parents, one or both, and you as a child. See your parents, one or both of them, criticizing and attacking you in some way so that you felt threatened and upset. Hear the verbal as well as the nonverbal messages. Notice what that child heard and how the child's mind reacted to what it heard. What did the child decide it had to do to protect itself, to make sure the scene wouldn't happen again? Also, notice if the child accepted and internalized the parental messages, the judgments about what kind of child he or she was. How did that child feel? What did that child decide so that it would never feel that way again? Play the scene out. How did you respond as a child when you were threatened? What patterns did you create to protect yourself? Fine. Let the scene go off to the right.

And now, bring up the earliest scene you can recall in which you felt threatened, discounted, invalidated, or attacked as a person and as a human being. See yourself in that situation. Hear what was said. Notice how your mind responded. Did it decide: "I'm never going to think that again" or "I'm going to block it out" or "I'm going to make them wrong, if they're going to make me wrong" or "I'll reject them before they can reject me"? Look into the heart and mind of that child, and listen to the thoughts of that child. Play the scene out; see it clearly; stay conscious. Stay in your observer. And notice what the child concluded, what he or she secretly believed about himself or herself. Notice the decision made by the child.

And now, be aware of how you later expressed that decision in your relationships, in your way of being in the world. Observe the defensive patterns you've used to keep you unaware of that decision and those feelings. Consider what that cost you in terms of your ability to love, to be alive, to be joyful.

Let that scene go off to the right. And from the left, bring up a scene, in which your mother was threatened or discounted, and watch how she reacted to that attack. Notice how she reacted to that threat. If you can, enter her mind, and imagine what she thought about herself and about that other person. How did she react? Is there any similarity between her reaction, her defense patterns, and yours? Play out the scene, seeing her defend against that perceived threat. Notice any similarities between your defense patterns and hers. And then, let that scene go off to the right.

Repeat the process with your father. From the left, bring up a scene, in which your father was criticized or attacked. Notice how he defended. Did he attack back? Did he make the other person wrong? Did he withdraw or hide? If you can, look into his mind and perceive his thoughts and feelings. Notice any similarity between the way you defend and the way he defended, between the way you resist and the way he resisted.

There are two things I'd like you to be clear about and understand in this process. First, what is your negative ground-of-being decision? What is the deeply buried belief about yourself that you assumed as a child? Second, how did you structure your life, your mind patterns, your games, so that you avoided awareness of that decision? How did you decide to resist it?

When you're ready, reorient yourself to the room. And open your eyes.

Your Negative Ground-of-Being

Through the meditation, you became aware of the primary negative decision you made about yourself as a child, based on your negative experiences with your parents on what they said was true about you. From then on, you assumed those evaluations of yourself as your negative ground-of-being, upon which you developed positions about yourself and the world.

In addition, you saw the ways you avoided being aware of the initial hurt, anger, or fear associated with your negative ground-of-being. The patterns you developed out of that original decision about yourself formed your defense structure, which you used then and continue to use now to avoid awareness of that decision.

Remember that your mind's purpose or design function is the survival of your tapes, your beliefs, including your negative ground-of-being decision. Remember also that you can operate from two realms, the ordinary and the extraordinary. Your mind's promotion of your negative ground-of-being, along with the avoidance patterns you built upon that foundation, keep you in the ordinary universe and make you unaware of the extraordinary possibilities within you and the world.

In the ordinary universe, you operate from your training and conditioning. And that is what excludes from your life the possibility of experiencing joy, love, intimacy, caring, contact.

How did you set up this unreal reality, in which you must live? How is it that you came to believe that your present, mostly miserable, experience is the real thing? How can you know, then, what is real? With the process as a catalyst, consider how your mind patterns began, and how they operate in your relationships with self and others.

Direct Experience vs. Belief

The only way you can know anything is through your experience. But remember that your mind processes your experiences according to your tapes and patterns. And so, it dilutes the direct experience of "out there." Through your mind, you internalize the experience, process it through your perceptual filters, and then project it onto the world as something different. It is no longer the direct experience.

You can be aware in two ways: through your direct experience, and through your beliefs. (See Model 3.1.) When you first encounter "X," you have the opportunity to experience "X" as it exists in universe. You experience "X" first through specific sensory stimulation—through your sense of touch, smell, taste, hearing, and sight. Your experience of "X" through your senses leads to general sensory stimulation and engages your peripheral and central nervous systems, through which your body responds involuntarily to "X." In the third stage of direct experience, your mind describes the experience by making an imprint of the specific and general sensory pattern as you react to "X." In other words, your mind, as a linear arrangement of total, multi-sensory recording of successive moments of here and now, makes a recording of "X."

Our Tape System as a Filter

At this point, you move away from the direct experience. You leave your natural knowing of "X" and filter the experience of it through your ego; you evaluate, critique, and judge your experience of "X." Your mind assesses the original experience through your tape system, so the purity of "X," as a direct experience, is lost in the debris of your beliefs.

MODEL 3.1   TWO WAYS TO BE AWARE

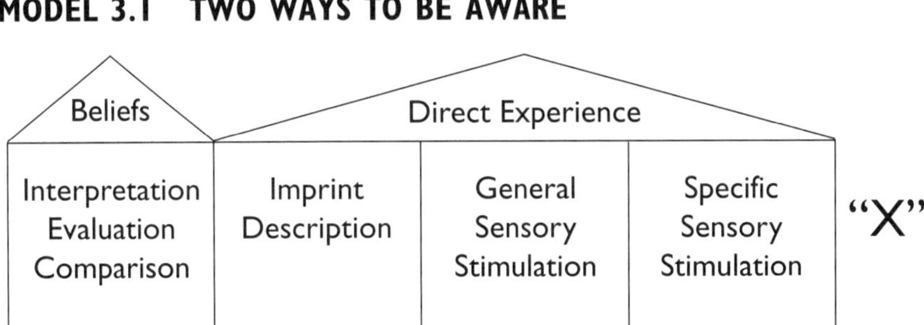

In the beginning, an experience is full, complete. There is nothing you need to add to it. For example, your original experience of a relationship partner is adequate and satisfying. But, when you filter your direct experience of your partner through your beliefs, your mind decides, out of its negative ground-of-being, that the relationship, the person, is not enough. At that point, you impose demands, expectations, and manipulations on your partner. And because you believe that the person is not enough or not okay, your experience of the relationship with that person becomes not okay as well. Your mind uses your beliefs about yourself and the relationship to help you avoid the pain that you too may not be enough; you avoid the awareness of your negative ground-of-being.

Why does the mind filter your direct experience? The mind promotes the survival of your tapes, including your negative ground-of-being so that when you have a direct and positive experience of a relationship, your mind, out of its need to uphold your tapes, filters the experience so that a positive experience becomes negative. Your mind perceives the possibility of a positive experience as a contradiction to your negative ground-of-being, as a threat. The mind needs to be right, so it uses defense mechanisms to distort the experience; the negative belief survives.

The other person and the relationship are initially whole and complete, and you are whole and complete in it. But to the mind, wholeness and completeness refute your negative ground which says you are inadequate, that you don't deserve the positive experience of yourself and someone else. The mind distorts the experience so that it validates your negative ground-of-being, and invalidates the direct experience.

For example, imagine that at work, you speak to and walk toward a coworker. But the coworker seems indifferent, and, in fact, turns and walks away from you. The direct experience is simply that your coworker walks away.

However, your mind perceives your coworker's actions as a threat,

Creating Your Act

P: If I have a negative ground-of-being that says I'm inadequate, how does that make the other person wrong?

Tony: Let's say that as a child, I do not receive recognition or acceptance for being myself. What evaluation or judgment do you think I will make about me?

P: You'll do something else to get attention.

Tony: Okay. But, specifically, what will I decide about me?

P: That I'm not all right.

Tony: Yes, who I am isn't enough. And as a result of that decision, I eliminate the possibility of power, competence, joy; I eliminate the possibility of experiencing myself as okay, because I believe I'm not okay. Of course, I don't want to experience myself as not okay. So, how can I avoid the experience of not being okay? What's the solution?

P: Make everybody else not okay.

Tony: Yes, that's a specific game solution, but basically what do I have to do?

P: *Be somebody else.*

Tony: Exactly. I have to be somebody else, and so I *create my act.*

as rejection. Your mind construes the experience as a second-degree upset; you are threatened with a perceived loss. The threat activates the mind's survival function since loss ultimately implies abandonment and death. And so, through your mind, you assume a defensive position which makes you, on the surface, right, and the other person wrong.

The Mind Is Smart, But Unaware

How could the mind, in its intelligence, believe that your negative ground-of-being could be right? The mind doesn't necessarily promote the survival of the self, but rather the survival of what the self considers itself to be. It fosters the survival of your tapes. The mind is not smart in the sense of being aware. It lacks wisdom, which is a function of the self. The mind is a machine; it doesn't consider the validity or usefulness of the tape. It only records the tape and then, out of its design function, ensures its continuation.

So, externally, you deny there's anything wrong with you. But, within, out of your negative ground-of-being, you believe you are not okay. On the surface, you defend against being wrong, through the mind. But through your defending, you separate yourself from the extraordinary universe, from your self, so that your mind can make your negative ground-of-being be true.

As a biocomputer, your mind is only as good as the data you put into it. If you input "1+1=3," then the computer will always print out "1+1=3." When you compile your tapes as a child, you are not smart enough to know that "1+1=2." And if "1+1=3" is already there, that is what you believe is true.

You can only perceive what you can conceive. Initially, your perceptions are direct, but as they are filtered through the model, the experience becomes just another concept. As you live, you filter additional experiences, adding on so that your mind buries the original experience.

For example, take a moment to look around the room and notice everything in the room that is white. Now close your eyes, and think of everything that is black in this room. Okay, now open your eyes. You didn't see what was black, because, earlier, you focused your awareness on everything that was white.

Acts: How We Make Them and Break Them

Since we don't want to experience ourselves as not okay, we create ways to be somebody else—someone who is okay. We create acts for ourselves. Your ego orchestrates your act. It decides what you will include in your act so that you can experience yourself as okay. For example, I might cultivate my appearance as part of my act; I might spend time promoting an image of myself through my clothes, my hair, my car. Or I might project an image based on my behavior; I decide to be very nice or very tough. And for a while, my act works.

My act breaks down when I begin to perceive myself as really okay. When I begin to feel I'm okay, I am violating the tape that says I'm not. The act becomes stale, inadequate, meaningless. The car I bought as part of my act no longer seems exciting. So, I have to trade it and buy a newer, sportier one. And then, soon, the new car seems unexciting as well, because my mind insists that I'm not okay. It continually refers to my negative ground-of-being. And the mind begins to make my experience of myself as not okay a reality.

Think of some examples of people who have had wonderful acts, so wonderful that millions of people loved them—and yet, they were unable to experience that love themselves so they eventually killed themselves. Elvis Presley and Marilyn Monroe are good examples. You find the most blatant acts in Hollywood. Everybody loves a movie star, but if the star doesn't feel loved inside, the star has to create it or replace it with something else, such as drugs or a string of intimate relationships.

Such people think someone else can make them whole. It's like trying to hang on to a handful of water: The tighter you hold it, the more rapidly you lose it. As long as you operate under the illusion that someone else can make you whole—which implies that you are incomplete—you operate from your negative ground-of-being, which is reinforced by your mind. You build your life around that early negative decision about yourself.

Protecting Your Negative Ground-of-Being

Let's say you begin as a golden coin, perfect and complete, valuable and valued. Then, you add your negative ground-of-being decision; you stack it on top of the original gold coin. And then, you add other coins, life experiences, stacking them precariously, one on top of the other. You cover not only the original bright coin at the bottom (your self), but also the tarnished second coin (your negative ground-of-being). Each coin or experience added skews the stack (your life), making it wobbly and unstable.

On the physical level, the process resembles a reaction to a hip injury: You compensate for the pain in your hip by twisting your body. You favor the hip (your negative ground-of-being), thus, throwing your body (your life) off balance. Parts of it atrophy, while others remain undeveloped. If you compensate long enough, you develop curvature of the spine. Mentally, you compensate for your negative ground-of-being through defense mechanisms, which weaken your sense of self and distort your direct experience.

In the meditation, you experienced the original psychic injury, along with your mind's reactions to it. And as you listened to the attack, you consciously denied it, resisted it, struggled mightily against the truth of it.

I say the truth, because secretly, in your heart, when your mother or father, the goddess and god of your child's universe, communicated that you were unlovable, stupid, and inadequate, you protested, and yet, you also believed them. So, while you ran for cover through your defense mechanisms, you also bought into what they said. When you were told you weren't enough, you defended yourself, while your mind recorded the information as fact. And it is your mind, through your negative ground-of-being decision, that organizes your life so that you play out or act out of your tape. If you believe you are not enough, then you will create that in your relationships, while at the same time, you defend against it by making the other person wrong.

For example, in the beginning of a relationship, you feel good. The relationship seems complete. After awhile, however, the other person turns out to be imperfect, and you reject him. Then he rejects you, and you return to your negative ground-of-being as the truth. Your mind sets it up.

Denial as a Defense Mechanism

What are some of the defense structures of the mind? How does the mind defend itself so that it can always be dominant or right? How does your mind validate its position? How does it make the other person wrong?

Your mind denies the existence of what it wishes to avoid. You can block out pieces of your own body, awareness of parts of your body. Of course, you also can block out awareness of emotions.

Some people deny positives. Their parents described the world as dog-eat-dog, a belief that became the child's negative ground. Then, when someone offers them a warm fuzzy, they interpret it as a con; they suspect that someone wants something from them. So they deny the experience of the warm fuzzy for what it is—unconditional love.

Repression as a Defense Mechanism

Others deny negatives; they assume a sunny-side-up position. As children, they couldn't complain or exhibit strong emotions. And so they deny the negative; they deny pain, hurt, anger. But, whenever you deny or resist the negative—the anger, for instance—it festers and grows. Whenever their anger surfaces, they repress it. And whenever they witness someone else's anger, they have to deny that too because it resonates with their own repressed anger and scares them. They fear other's anger as well as their own. So, they use denial and repression to avoid it.

Dealing with Anger

Remember that you have one foot in the extraordinary universe, the realm of awareness and experience. At the same time, you must keep the other foot in the ordinary universe, where you are human. And as a human being, you get angry from time to time. Realize that you are human, and at the same time, you are god; you can be angry, and yet, also be above your anger. Don't deny and repress your anger; instead, practice being above it by accepting your anger as a normal part of your human structure.

If you deny and repress it, you inevitably will express it in other, less aware ways. For example, your anger may be expressed psychosomatically through your body, through illness and disease. Or you may play it out in your relationships through passive aggressive behavior or withdrawal.

Anger is a process, the mind's process. You, as self, have a choice. Either you can let it hook you as you play it out with yourself or with others, or, as an aware, enlightened person, you can accept it. You can be big enough to allow yourself to be where you are.

If you recognize where the anger is coming from, from your mind, and you don't deny it, will it go away? It will go away in the sense that you allow yourself to experience it out. We all have these feelings, beliefs, and mind tapes that will surface as the mind attempts to dominate and control our experience. But, you have the choice. You can choose your approach. You can operate from your ego, from your defenses, or you can choose to come from your awareness, from your

---

Crazy or crazy in love?

Tony: I have a friend who met someone and fell in love with her. He accepted her unconditionally. Do you know what her reaction was?

P: She thought he was crazy.

Tony: Right. She couldn't imagine why he loved her, because she didn't love herself. She had an unlovable tape, so she couldn't believe someone loved her unconditionally. So, she had to make him wrong; she had to prove that he didn't really love her. And she withdrew, shut down, because she believed she didn't deserve that kind of love. And so, she made the tape come true; she ended up feeling unloved.

P: So, how would you begin to untangle that pattern?

Tony: First, be aware of your tapes. And then, whenever they run, just listen. Allow yourself to feel the loss, the fear, but don't buy into it. Don't believe it and don't act on it. And realize that other people operate out of their own experience, not out of yours. They, like you, do the best they can, given their negative ground-of-being and tape system.

experience, your purpose, your self. When you attempt to freeze yourself, your relationships, through manipulations and defensive games, you eliminate the possibility of direct experience. You replace it with a form, based on your mind's patterns, which you impose on your experience. If you believe that your life is tragic and that you are a victim, then you will project that belief onto your life and relationships.

Projection as a Defense Mechanism

Projection is one of the mind's most significant and destructive defense mechanisms. Actually, everything is a projection, even the positive experiences. You create your total experience. Through projection, you take a part of you—a belief, a feeling, an experience—and paint the world with it. You organize your life, not around your actual experience, but around your mind and its tapes, its beliefs about the way things are or should be.

Typically, we project the parts of ourselves we most want to avoid. If we deny and repress anger, then that is what we see in others. We don't see it in ourselves, and yet, it exists, so we project it out onto others. We can do the same thing with fear; we see fear in another person and we focus on their fear as a way not to see our own.

Fear and anger are not defense mechanisms. They are emotions that run your machinery. Fear and anger, when you resist them, can act as catalysts for the mind to begin to defend. Strong emotions trigger the mind's survival mechanism.

Blemishing as a Defense Mechanism

Another defense mechanism that we use to be right and make someone else wrong is blemishing. Through blemishing, you focus critically on appearances or personality traits, to diminish others. You diminish your experience of them, by criticizing the way they look or act, so that you can be one-up. You can be right. You avoid characteristics you don't like about yourself, and then, project them onto someone else. Whenever you find yourself criticizing someone else, turn it around and say it about yourself. And discover the truth of it within you.

Rationalization as a Defense Mechanism

Rationalization is a common and powerful method for defining your reality, or distorting your reality and denying your experience. Through rationalization, you explain, justify, excuse.

Through rationalization, you reduce the threat that you may be wrong, which your mind interprets as a threat to your survival. The mind distorts reality and turns failure into victory. At the same time, you turn victory into failure, because your aware self knows your mind is lying.

Procrastination as a Defense Mechanism

Through procrastination, you avoid your fear of failure or success. By delaying action, you defend against possible failure, and in the positive sense, against possible success, if you believe you cannot succeed.

Introjection as a Defense Mechanism

Through introjection, you internalize. For example, you may internalize your mother's criticism of you. Mom doesn't even have to be present. You do it; you attack yourself.

Sublimation as a Defense Mechanism

Through sublimation, you take the belief that it's not okay for you to pleasure yourself, to feel good about yourself, and you use the belief to be miserable. Whenever you experience pleasurable feelings, associated with sex, love, affection, you twist and distort those feelings. You can't accept the pleasure, so instead, you become a person who pleases others.

The distortion of our sexuality illustrates the sublimation process. When you begin to feel loving and sexual at puberty, and you become involved with someone and begin to express those sexual feelings, initially it feels wonderful. But, since you're not allowed to experience pleasure, you deny it through tapes that present your sexuality as bad or wrong. You sublimate those self-pleasure, sexual feelings; you don't give yourself permission to have them.

Pleasers and Takers

Still, it has to be expressed, so you become a pleaser. You take those feelings and deny them for yourself, and instead, put your energy into pleasuring someone else. You pick out a taker, so that you can express those feelings, while secretly, you hope that through your pleasing, the taker will eventually please you. In reality, you end up pleasing and pleasing, while the taker continues taking. Finally, you become angry, because you feel like a victim. Examples of pleasers include super mom, super nurse, big daddy—all roles that accelerate pleasing behavior while the child within screams that it's miserable. You feel unfulfilled, dissatisfied, inadequate, unloved—which is what you feared and what you hoped to avoid.

Experience Your Unexperienced Experiences

As you move through your barriers, as you drop your defenses, you will experience an enormous amount of fear because you are facing the terror of non-survival. We struggle to avoid death, and yet, we always end up with what we seek to avoid. Ultimately, we die a little each day. The more you resist dying, the more you will end up with the experience of dying. And the deadness radiates beyond your physical body; you become emotionally dead as well.

So, how do you get beyond fear? You begin to experience out your unexperienced experiences. Bring up that fear that, as a child, you thought would kill you. Shine a flashlight, your awareness, on it, and discover that you can be afraid and be perfect at the same time. You can be afraid and powerful, so powerful that the fear can exist, can be, while it ceases to run your life. The loser is the person who is so afraid that his fear paralyzes him. The winner, on the other hand, is also afraid, but he goes on.

Look at what paralyzes you. Look at how you resist. When someone attacks you or criticizes you, you can react in two ways. First you can resist it, but your very resistance makes the criticism and the fear a reality. Whatever you resist in you persists.

On the other hand, you can handle criticism from the position of the aware self. Realize that someone's criticism is a function of where they are and has nothing to do with you. Don't take it personally. Don't defend against their defense.

Whatever You Resist Persists

Actually on an introductory level, there are two steps to transcending your mind, to being bigger than the fear:

◆ **Give up your resistance.** Just be with the criticism and all the feelings it brings up. Do nothing about it; don't act on it. Be willing to give up your resistance to that other person, which means you give up your attachment to what they think and to what your mind tells you you should do about what they think or say. Allow the other person to be where they are.

◆ **Check your purpose.** Use what they've said to achieve your own purpose. Be clear about why you're interacting with that person, about what you are attempting to accomplish in the relationship. And then use it, all of it, the good and the bad, to move yourself forward, toward awareness rather than backwards into ego.

Martin Luther King was a master at using other people's resistance to achieve his purpose. He allowed the racist to be a racist, while he continued his pursuit. He didn't defend; he transformed through awareness and peace, rather than through ego and violence.

Criticism as a Gift

For now, practice being the observer. Watch how your mind functions, how you create reality out there. Disconnect yourself from the attachments that are based on your negative ground. Be with whatever you experience. Be bigger than what your mind tells you. And then, keep moving forward toward transformation. If you keep moving, even though you feel like giving in and be-lieving what they're saying about you, you will discover that there's more than enough love out there. There are four billion people in the world. Why cut yourself off because someone insults you or because you think they don't love you the way you want to be loved?

Use the criticism as a frame for your purpose. Look at it as a gift, as an opportunity to come from the extraordinary universe while living in

---

How to make nonresistance work for you

P: Are you saying then that you should turn the other cheek, just let people walk all over you?

Tony: No, the process of nonresistance requires conscious action, not passivity. You don't lie down with "Walk On Me" stenciled on your shirt. You do nothing in the sense that you don't defend.

P: Let's say that the other person criticizes or attacks. Then, you let that person be critical and you realize their criticism has nothing to do with you. Where does the power and the action come in? It still seems passive to me.

Tony: The power springs from your aware self, the part of you that is bigger than what someone else says, the part of you that knows you are perfect. You go with it rather than oppose it. You don't get caught in the cross and counter flows of other people's mind games. You use those people and their comments to move you forward.

P: So, you use other people's games to practice nonresistance, to make contact with your aware self, so that you stay on purpose?

Tony: Yes. If you use your tapes as a response to their tapes, you will lock in on their level, thus slowing down your evolution, your forward movement.

---

the ordinary universe. After all, the universe is rich and full and loving, and you can make that your projection. You can create it any way you want. You've created your world the other way—as inadequate, unloving, incomplete. You are god in your universe, so create it the way you want to experience it.

Sing it

Life is your song to sing—Sing it
sing it now
sing it here
sing it softly
sing it loudly
sing it as you wish
only
Sing it
sing it for you
because it enriches you
sing it for me
because it enriches me
only
Sing it

Game Playing

Guided Fantasy

Close your eyes now. Get comfortable. And begin to breathe; focus on breathing deeply and slowly. And when you feel totally relaxed, begin to move into your meditative space, your safe space. Go to that place in whatever way seems easiest. And then, rest there, moving into your center.

When you feel centered, take a few moments to think about your relationships, especially about the games you play in those relationships. Think back over the past week; remember any confrontations, any discussions which left you feeling bad about yourself and about the relationship. What game did you play with that person or with those people? What games did they play with you?

Fine. When you can remember a few games, focus on one specific encounter you had in the last week. Recreate the beginning of the encounter with this other person; how did it start?

Notice the verbal and nonverbal communication between the two of you. Watch the interaction up to the point where you felt uncomfortable, where you experienced a negative emotion. Notice what the other person said to you that triggered that negative emotional state within you. What did that other person say or do that started the game process? Did that person say something about you? Did they ignore you? Or did they disagree with you? What exactly triggered your need to play a game with that person?

Just be there with that awareness for a moment. Now, still in your observer position, notice how your mind, body, and emotions reacted to the trigger. First, become aware of what your mind was thinking after the trigger. What did your mind say to you? What did it tell you about that other person? And then, notice what your mind said about you. How did your mind take that trigger and reflect it back onto you, back to your negative ground-of-being decision?

Fine. And now, become aware of your body. How did your body react? How did your body respond to the trigger, and then to the mind's judgments about you and the other person? Do a body scan, and notice where you feel tense. Notice any pain or discomfort in your body. Become aware of any physical sensations.

Good. And now connect with your emotional self. What did you feel during the confrontation? What did you feel about what the other person said or did? How did you feel about yourself? And then, go even deeper and get in touch with any other emotions. What were they? Were you afraid? Be aware of your feelings, your body sensations, your thoughts.

Now, put yourself back into the situation, back into the confrontation or discussion with the other person. And notice how you acted out those thoughts, sensations, and feelings. How did you react? Notice first how you reacted emotionally. How did you cover up your fear? With anger?

And then, notice how you acted out the cover. What did you do? What actions did you take to avoid your fear and anger? Notice your behavior; focus on the set of behaviors you used to avoid your anger and fear, to avoid the trigger that started the whole process. What was your act?

And then, become aware of your game again. What thoughts did you use to justify or rationalize your position, your game? How did you make it okay to play your game?

Fine. You have completed a cycle; you have returned to the beginning of a closed, cybernetic loop. (See Model 4.1 on page 70.) The cycle began with a trigger to which you reacted. And you reacted through and with your machinery; you responded with your mind, through your body, and out of your feelings. Then, in an attempt to avoid those feelings, you created an act, a set of behaviors designed to cover up the fear, anger, and especially, your negative ground-of-being. Out of your act, you devised games to protect you from awareness, to keep you in unawareness.

And finally, you complete the cycle where it began: in your mind. Through your mind, you excused, justified, or rationalized your game. You made the other person wrong, and yourself right. You won. Or did you?

Anatomy of a Game

Let's say the game began when your boss complained about the way you do your job. The trigger for the game was your boss' comment that he would have to do the job himself, in order to get it done right. His comments trigger reactions in your mind, body, and emotions.

The Mind's Reaction

Look at Model 4.1, beginning with the mind. What did you think about your boss after he said that? Did you think he was being unfair? Then, you probably started an internal dialogue in which you muttered: "Why is he blaming me? He shouldn't be talking to me that way. I did the best I could . . ." What did you end up thinking about yourself? Perhaps you decided you were worthless. You returned to your negative ground-of-being—which in this case was your worthlessness.

The Body's Reaction

Meanwhile, how did your body react to the situation, to the trigger, and to the thoughts? What happened to you physically? Perhaps your stomach began to feel tight. You had trouble breathing. Your body reacted by tightening up.

MODEL 4.1   BARRIER TO AWARENESS

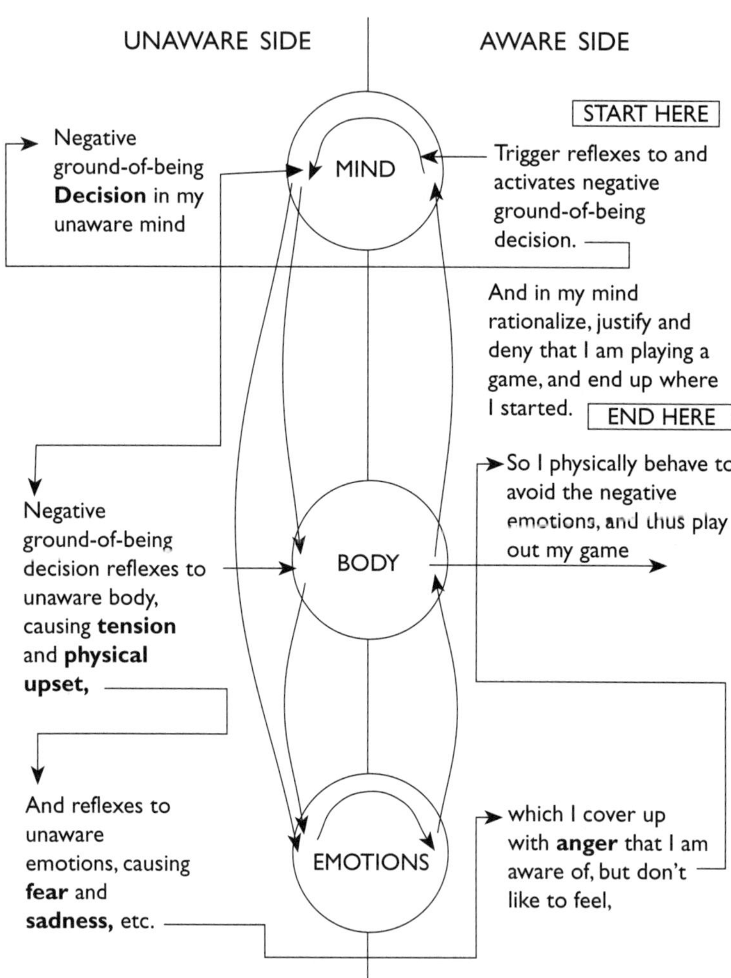

The Emotional Reaction

How do your boss' remarks make you feel? Do you feel afraid? Aside from the practical fear of losing your job, you probably also experienced a fear of rejection. Your mind told you that you weren't good enough.

And then, you probably thought to yourself, "What if he finds out I really am unworthy?"

At that point, you began your cover-up. How did you hide your fear of being fired, of being rejected? You got angry and indignant. You began to puff up and got red in the face. You replaced the uncomfortable feeling of fear with the feeling of power—with anger.

But what did you do next? You were filled with angry energy and had no place to discharge it. What did you do?

Looking at the model, you reascended the stages, beginning with your emotions: on the left side of the model, you felt fear; when you moved to the right side of the model, you changed the fear to anger. And then you moved back up to your body, where you acted out your feelings through your behavior.

Creating an Act

You created an act to avoid your feelings of anger and fear, as well as your negative ground-of-being—worthlessness. You used your act to avoid the negative, to stay unaware. Out of your avoidance and your act came your game.

Playing a Game

You used the game to avoid the trigger, which in your case was criticism, as well as to avoid your mind's reaction to the criticism, which was fear. Of course, you didn't want to feel afraid and angry, so you played the game. In your case, you criticized your boss: He doesn't know what he's talking about. He made a mistake just last week. He's being unfair.

The negative emotion drives the game. It may be your sadness, your hurt, or your fear that drives your rejection game. Whatever inspires it, you reject them before they can reject you.

But, you create a paradox: whatever you avoid through the game will be what you end up with. In other words, while you play a game to avoid rejection—when you reject them before they reject you—you still end up feeling alone, unlovable, and rejected.

Game Alert: Negative Payoff

In fact, your game payoff can alert you to the fact that you're playing a game. Remember that the game has a trigger; it is triggered by what the other person says or does; their actions activate your internal pattern. Through the game, you and the other person move, dance, until you receive your payoff, which is always a negative emotion. So, use your emotional state as a gauge, as a red flag which can signal your game.

And so, you complete the cybernetic cycle. You end up where you started: in your mind. From your mind, you excuse, justify, and rationalize your game. For example, you might rationalize your criticism of your boss by blaming it on the fact that he attacked you first. You assume a position and then rationalize it.

Game Positions

There are three positions you can play in any game: rescuer, victim, or persecutor. Let's examine these positions by studying the dynamics of a few games.

Persecutor

Let's start with a popular game: NIGYSOB or Now I've Got You S.O.B. This is a one-up game, in which you play the persecutor. You set

---

Getting Even

P: I tend to play the victim. And after I've been used, I tend to retaliate quietly. I mean I don't say much but I find ways to make it difficult for the persecutor.

Tony: That's called passive aggressive behavior, which is a type of game behavior. It begins with anger, which you cannot overtly express to your boss. So you sit with it, hold it in, for a while. You may not even be aware of it when you accidentally switch those figures on the report he has to present to the board next week. And you feel badly, sort of, when he reads the report, realizes the figures are mixed up, and looks incompetent.

---

the other person up so that he or she ends up failing, and you can persecute that person. It's a common game in corporations. However, in order for someone to play NIGYSOB, you need a willing partner.

Let's say a supervisor asks Joe to complete a project in three weeks with no assistance. In reality, the project would take three people six weeks to finish. But Joe doesn't say anything, at the time. However, at the end of three weeks, he has to tell his boss he hasn't completed the project. Of course, his boss knew he would never be able to; nevertheless, he nails Joe to the wall. NIGYSOB.

Victim

What about Joe? What game did he play? What happened to him? He was victimized by the boss. He played Kick Me, in which he assumed a one-down, victim position as a response to his boss.

Actually Joe had a choice. He could have responded to his supervisor in two ways. He could have responded the way he did, by matching NIGYSOB with Kick Me, or he could have refused to play the game. You always have that choice. You can let the game be there. Let the other person play it, but then, refuse to take the bait. In other words, you don't accept an assignment under terms which guarantee your failure. You assert your need.

You don't have to put yourself psychologically in a victim position unless you enjoy being there. Some people do enjoy being one-down. They get a lot of mileage out of being victimized: They can discredit their supervisors at work; they can wallow in self-pity; they can complain about management without having to be responsible for changing the situation—either by refusing to play the game or by moving on to another job.

Rescuers

Rescuers play Look How Hard I Tried, or I Was Only Trying To Help. Many times, the rescuer becomes the victim, especially when no one takes his advice. Or he assumes the role of persecutor—"I told you so!"

You can assume any one of the roles, and even change positions in the middle of a game. Actually, underneath all three of these roles hides a person who feels he's been victimized.

For example, when I justify persecuting you, I claim, "You let me down. What's wrong with you? Why can't I ever depend on anybody?" The persecutor's perceived victimization excuses his anger toward you. So, the righteous, superior, aggressive type feels just as victimized as the Kick Me player. Both blame other people for their feelings of helplessness or unworthiness.

Both the NIGYSOB player and the Kick Me player make the same negative ground-of-being decision: They believe they can't make it. And they're afraid that that's the truth. So, they use the game to defend or protect themselves. And then, they rationalize the game, and the mind uses it to keep them locked in the loop and in their unawareness.

Recently, I counseled a couple who nicely illustrate the rationalization game. In my office, the wife begins by saying to her husband, "Listen, whenever I tell you how I feel, I don't feel like you understand me at all." And he says, "Well, what about last week when you told me you felt like having dinner, and I asked you where you'd like to go?" (As you can see, we already have a win-lose situation. They're already locked into their positions.)

Still, she tries again, "You don't have to excuse or justify. All I want you to do is listen to me." He says, "I'm not excusing or justifying. I can give you lots of examples when I listen." (Of course, this is not one of those examples.)

As soon as she shares that she doesn't feel heard by him, he immediately defends, excuses, and justifies. He blocks out his ability to be aware of himself, of her, and of their relationship.

You can use your machinery—your mind, body, and emotions—to enhance rather than to block your experience. Most of us lock into the last step, into our minds, by justifying the games we play. And so, we eliminate much of our ability to experience. In this case, the husband blocked out his opportunity to really hear what his wife was saying, not just through his ears, but, more importantly, from his heart.

When you continue to excuse and justify your games, you inevitably begin the cycle again. Your defending catapults you back into your negative ground-of-being, because at some level, you know you are conning yourself with your excuses.

The Loop: One Man's Dilemma

Unconsciously, the husband knew he wasn't hearing her; he also knew that he was feeling inadequate. His defending triggered his negative ground-of-being decision, which made him feel even more inadequate. Meanwhile, he's thinking to himself: "She says mean things to me." And then, he thinks about how mean she is; and he believes the reason she must be so mean to him is that he really must be inadequate. At that point, his chest constricts and his stomach hurts, which makes him feel afraid, which he has to cover up with his fury. Then he acts indignant and moves into playing a defensive game. Finally, he excuses himself by saying, "What else can I do? I have this mean wife . . . and she is soooo mean . . ."

He continues defending, and he feels more inadequate because he has to excuse and justify, which makes his stomach tighter, which scares him even more, which makes him even angrier, which makes him want to avoid all of it, so he plays a game, which he has to then justify . . . And so it goes when you're caught up in the loop. He continues his circular journey, never hearing her, and always feeling inadequate.

In his negative ground-of-being, the husband believes he is inadequate, although he is unaware that he believes that about himself. So, he has to create an act that demonstrates how adequate he is; this is the cover up. Then, when someone says "you're inadequate," their comments activate his fear that he is inadequate. And he moves through the cycle until he arrives at his act and his game again. He uses his act to defend against awareness of his negative ground-of-being.

Getting Out of the Vicious Cycle

How and where do you exit from the closed loop pattern? What's the first step out of the trap?

◆ **Give up your excuses, rationalizations, and justifications.** Remember what your mind is; remember its purpose. Consider its function and how it keeps you locked into your position of righteousness, which in the beginning, is your belief in your negative ground-of-being. At the deepest level, you believe you are unlovable or inadequate and that's the original position your mind tries to protect. In this step, you accept the feelings; don't struggle against them.

◆ **Don't believe your mind.** You handle the game externally, out there in your relationships and at work, and you handle it internally, from your awareness of your self. Don't attach yourself to the game, to what your mind tells you is true. Step back into your observer, into your aware self, and realize that your mind wants to hook you. In this step, you give up your games.

◆ **Use your mantra and meditation.** Remember that through meditation, you can avoid, even transcend the hook. Meditation leads you out of your mind and into your awareness, where you can observe the mind as it creates the lies you base your life on.

What happens when you don't buy into the mind's lies? What does your awareness expose you to? You see your game. When you stop rationalizing your games, you become aware of them. And then when you stop playing the game, what will you encounter?

Create Positive Payoff Games

You have to create new games in which you receive a positive payoff. When you give up your games, you open up new possibilities; you open yourself to the potential to create in your life something new, something that you want. You build new patterns so that you can build your life, your relationships, the way you want.

Experiencing and Expressing Anger

Returning to the model, what will happen when you recognize and relinquish your game? You will backtrack to unravel the closed loop. The next time someone criticizes you, resist running your game, and try to come from center. Eventually, you'll reexperience your anger.

In the past, you expressed your anger through your game. But now, you sit with it; you still feel the anger, but you don't act it out. You be big enough to allow the feelings to be there, to allow yourself to experience whatever is there, rather than playing it out in a game that harms you or the relationship.

Handling soft emotions, like sadness and grief, is easier. Instead of

When guilt is the payoff

P: What if all you get is guilt when you give up the game and try to create new, fun ones, with positive payoffs?

Tony: First, consider the dynamics of your relationship game. What does he say that triggers you and your games? And then, what do you do and say, and finally, what's the result?

P: I'm not clear about the game yet.

Tony: If you don't see it, if you're unaware of the game, you can't change it; you end up playing it out unconsciously.

You must first see the game to alter it. In your game, you're setting it up so that there are two alternatives: You can get angry at him or you can feel guilty about not getting angry at him, because you think you should be angry at him. Look at the triggers or moves in the game that make you end up with the payoff of feeling guilty. Then you will be able to take the second step, which is giving up the old game and creating a new one.

P: It's a game in which one of us is going to win and the other is going to lose.

Tony: Well, ultimately, in a game, both of you lose by winning. You win by receiving your game payoff; yet, you lose because your payoff is negative. You end up with guilt and anger.

Look at how you would rather experience you and how you would rather experience him. Then, look at how you can create the new experience in place of the old experience of anger and guilt.

P: Well, it seems to me that if I stop playing the game, if I give up the anger, I'll end up with guilt, at least for a while.

Tony: So, what will you do with that guilt?

P: I'm not sure.

Tony: First, acknowledge that there's a little kid in you who's afraid she'll be hurt, rejected, and punished. Then look at your purpose in the relationship. How would you rather experience you, how would you like to feel about yourself and about your partner? And then, share with him. Point out the dynamics of the game, and tell him what you want instead. Ask for his suggestions on how to alter the pattern. Then both of you work together to create strategies for moving out of the old game.

acting those feelings out, you tend to internalize them. But we express our anger, a hard emotion, overtly. And when your anger reaches 5 or 6 on a scale of 0 to 10, it's more difficult to sit with it. Once the anger moves up to 6 on the scale, the emotion activates your physical system so that "being with it" is practically impossible.

Through awareness though, you can consciously express your anger. The criteria you use to express it so that you ultimately experience it out is: Don't hurt yourself and don't hurt anyone else.

When you choose not to punch someone's lights out, you might take away some of the satisfaction you used to experience in getting your anger out. But remember, you're enlightened now, so you go out into the backyard and chop wood. You can always pretend that so-and-so is the piece of wood. It will keep you out of jail. And it gets a lot of wood in for the winter.

So, find some physically strenuous activity through which you can express your anger. Whatever you do, express the anger consciously.

You Are Always at Choice

Since you are god in your own universe, you always have enough control to express your anger consciously. If you've got an anger problem, if your anger hurts your relationships and you, then plan, in advance, your strategy for handling your anger. You can use the Purpose Model on page 10. Decide specifically how you will handle your anger. What strategies will you use? You can use the same techniques to handle your fear—before you reach 6 or 7 on the scale.

So, give yourself permission to have your emotions. Give yourself the space to be where you are: to be unhappy, sad, afraid, alone, miserable. Be with your own truth, even if it is horrible, negative, scary. And when you do that, you'll end up facing your fear. You'll realize that you used the anger to conceal your fear—of rejection, of failure, of whatever.

Moving back up through the model, unraveling the loop, you'll become more aware of the physiological sensations you've been experiencing within the trap. You'll notice how you express or play out your anxiety through your ulcer or your migraine.

Returning to the Barrier

Ultimately, you will return to the barrier, the wall you've built through your games and defenses to avoid awareness of your negative ground-of-being. You learn to be bigger than the barrier. Allow yourself to feel what you feel. You become more centered, more conscious. Slowly the barrier will drop and, finally, you will face yourself—a centered, conscious being.

A centered person has moved back far enough, back to the barrier, so that he sees that he doesn't see. He is aware that he's unaware, and he recognizes the manifestations of his unawareness. He acknowledges it: He can afford to acknowledge it because he drops his defensive structure, which he used to protect himself from something that doesn't even exist.

What's the last plate in the armor suit you've been wearing all your life? You remember what the little kid in you decided long ago; you realize the decision you made as a child which started the whole process, which initiated the building of a defensive structure you thought you needed because you were afraid of abandonment, of lack of love, of death.

As we grew, we moved the barrier closer to our experience so that it became our experience; the wall then became our reality, our universe. So, in order to break the closed loop pattern, you have to cut through the cycle at the mind level. Only then, can you reclaim your experience and become the creator of a new extraordinary reality.

Aliveness

Aliveness is a function of
you seeing you
you hearing you
you tasting you
you touching you
you sensing you
so to experience aliveness
you see, hear, taste, touch, sense you
sense and be alive
non-sense and be dead

The Importance of Aliveness

Guided Fantasy

Close your eyes now. Inhale deeply. Fill your belly; expand your lungs. Breathe in, stretching, stretching. And then exhale, collapsing, emptying. Inhale deeply, filling, stretching. And then exhale, emptying. Inhale deeply again, filling, stretching, and then, exhale, emptying. Continue breathing deeply, stretching yourself, and then, emptying your lungs and belly completely. Breathe consciously and continuously for the next thirty minutes, while staying relaxed and observing your feelings, thoughts, and sensations.

Realize that your breathing can be a powerful tool for awareness. Through your breath, you may access repressed and unknown parts of yourself.

During the process, you may experience only your breathing; you may only be aware of the process of inhaling and exhaling. Or you may notice that your breathing affects parts of your body in varying degrees. Your face may become flushed, or your hands and feet will tingle. You may have a strong physiological reaction; you may feel pain in a particular area of your body; or, you may feel numb, as if parts of your body are missing or lifeless. You may even experience a lifting up out of your body.

You may experience emotional sensations or reactions. You may feel sad and even begin to cry. Your crying may be isolated, not triggered by any thought or feeling. You may feel fear or perhaps anger. As emotions surface, you may feel like sighing. Or you may have trouble breathing deeply. You may close down and hold your breath.

Continue to breathe fully and deeply. Fill your belly and then fill your chest. Then collapse and exhale. Then, fill your belly, fill your chest, and then empty out and collapse. Just observe whatever you feel or don't feel; be aware of any physical sensations or reactions; notice your thoughts. Stay with the process; be with it. Try to stay focused on breathing, rhythmically and deeply.

Your breathing and relaxation may activate your mind. As you move deeper into the experience of breathing, your mind may use defense mechanisms to keep you from being focused and aware. Don't focus on your mind or on your mantra. Focus only on your breathing. If your mind distracts you from your focal point, if you begin thinking about something or someone else, gently but firmly, bring your awareness back to your breathing. The only thing you have to do is to stay focused on the breathing and to be open to whatever thoughts, feelings, or sensations emerge.

The Value of Full Conscious Breathing

Most of us don't really breathe when we breathe. We may breathe a few times, or even for a few minutes. Then, we either hold our breath or breathe so shallowly that the process hardly resembles breathing.

The guided fantasy introduced you to the potential of real breathing and its effects on your organism. Through conscious and consistent breathing, you contact parts of yourself you usually avoid or are unaware of. In fact, the character of your breathing contributes to the degree and quality of your aliveness.

The Aliveness Scale

On an aliveness scale of minus 10 to plus 10, most of us operate around 2 or 3. If you experienced pain during the process, you rate close to a minus 10 on the scale of aliveness. If you felt or experienced little or nothing during the breathing, you may be described as one of the walking dead, which would place you at 0 on the scale; you may do a good imitation of aliveness, but your aware self knows it's just an act.

Probably few of us reached a plus 10, which would indicate full breathing, total aliveness. Most of us, when we breathe consciously, begin to move up the scale to 5 or 6. Breathing then offers us a way to reclaim the genuine experience of aliveness as a function of physical experiencing.

Your experiencing occurs in your body, so it follows that your body is the only place you can be alive. Your aliveness depends on more than genuine breathing. In fact, aliveness requires physical involvement in five areas: breathing, emotions, body movement, self-expression, and sexuality.

The Original You

Initially, you were all heart, all experience. (See Model 5.1 on page 84.) You were fully alive. You possessed and participated in the five components of your aliveness:

◆ **Breathing.** You breathed fully.

◆ **Emotions.** You loved freely.

◆ **Body movement.** You experienced your body as connected and whole.

Importance of aliveness

P: Can you be more active in some areas than in others and still be fairly alive?

Tony: Yes, but joyous living comes from a total experiencing of all five components. Otherwise, you live, but you are not fully alive.

P: Have we ever been completely alive?

Tony: Yes. In your infancy, you were alive in your experience. You experienced yourself as whole, complete, connected. You experienced joy, love, bliss directly. Your experience was unitary, an integrity of processes. Whatever happened to you, you—as an organism—responded totally.

◆ **Self-expression.** You knew what you felt and you willingly expressed it.

◆ **Sexuality.** You rejoiced in your sexuality.

MODEL 5.1. ALIVE PERSON

But then, you realized that your survival depended on someone else. You learned that, in spite of your connectedness, you were also separate. Soon, you felt safe only in the presence of someone else. Otherwise, you experienced separation anxiety; you knew in your heart, in your gut, that you depended on others to make it.

As you grew older, Mom and Dad increased their expectations and demanded that you do certain things, that you behave in certain ways. You feared that if you didn't meet those expectations, they might reject you, leave you; you would die because you needed them to survive.

The Experienced Experience

Actually, you did meet their expectations—for a while. At first, you responded to the expectation and satisfied it. As an organism, your bodily experience of your parents' expectations began in a relaxed state. You moved into a state of tension when you became aware of the expectation. Then, the mounting tension created a charge, a mental, emotional, physical buildup of energy. When you finally met the expectation, you discharged the energy. The discharge brought relief, since you could return to a state of relaxation.

You completed an experience. (See Model 5.2.)

However, at some point, you realized that, not only did you have to meet the here and now expectations, but also that more would come. Each day, in fact, brought more limits on what you did and how you behaved. Once, you could eat, sleep, eliminate whenever you wanted. That changed as the people you lived with expected you to live within their framework, as an extension of themselves and their lives. You began to feel you couldn't possibly satisfy all their expectations, and so your experience changed.

MODEL 5.2 EXPERIENCED EXPERIENCE

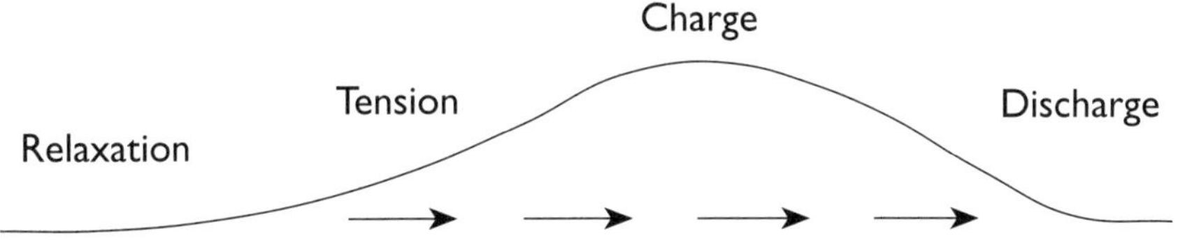

The Unexperienced Experience

Your fear about not meeting their demands activated your mind. Your mind and your ego began to operate for the survival of your tapes, beliefs, and values—all generated from your attempt to meet your parents' expectations. You moved out of and away from your bodily experience and into your mind, your ego. You lost the ability to completely relax and, instead, found yourself in a state of constant tension. The tension, as you tried to meet escalating expectations, increased and built up a charge.

However, you could no longer discharge the energy, because you could no longer meet all the expectations. (See Model 5.3 on page 86.)

And so, you began to accumulate a residue of ongoing tension in your body proportional to the accumulation of unexperienced experiences. You retreated to your mind to cut off your bodily experience, your total, organismic response. Because there was no discharge, you felt unremitting anxiety and developed an anxiety core. The core grew in proportion to the demands and your ability to meet them.

To protect itself from the frustration, the mind erected barriers which blocked your experience and inhibited your aliveness. Originally, your body functioned as a vehicle for your aliveness; over time, however, your body became the mind's storage shed for unexperienced experiences. The barriers created by the mind, the experiences locked out of your awareness, manifested as *body blocks.* Your experience, your aliveness, along with your expression of it, became distorted. Ultimately, your habitual response to other's expectations shaped your body, your behavior, and your experience of yourself and others.

MODEL 5.3 UNEXPERIENCED EXPERIENCE

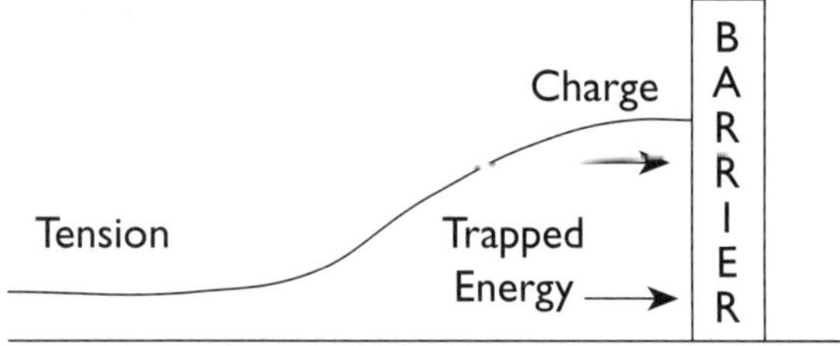

Experience vs. Ego

You withdrew your awareness of direct experience through your body and shifted the focus and the energy to your mind. Your original life in your experience (See Model 5.1 on page 84.) diminished as you moved toward an existence in your mind and ego. (See Model 5.4 on page 87.)

And so, you locked yourself in your mind's concepts, oblivious to the experience to your body. Because of your unhappiness, you retreated into autistic behavior, into fantasy. You developed an ego ideal, a positive fantasy about yourself, which denied your direct experience. You created the fantasy you thought would be most effective for denying the feelings and the parts of your body which interfered with your acceptance by Mom and Dad.

And so, the split between your ego and your experience divides you, fragments your aliveness. The ego wants power; it seeks to dominate, to be right, to make others wrong. In contrast, the body wants a full experience of pleasure, satisfaction, and completion. It seeks a discharge of experiential tension.

The discharge of energy brings release and genuine happiness—a physical, emotional experience in the body. Anything that interferes with that relaxation process—the building of tension, the charge, the discharge, the return to relaxation—anything that frustrates the body's completion of an experience, arouses feelings of helplessness, anxiety, and despair in you. The unexperienced experience keeps you from functioning as a whole and leads to segmentation.

MODEL 5.4 AUTISM

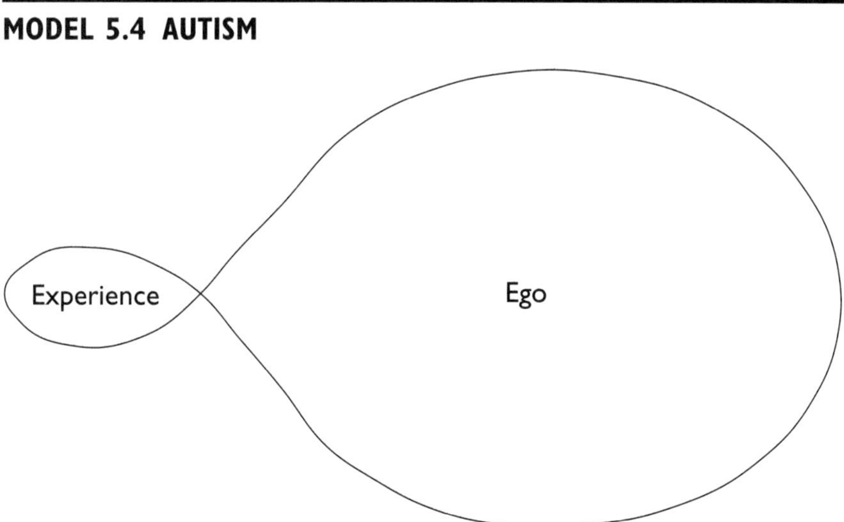

An unexperienced experience occurs in either of two ways: through a single major traumatic event, or through an insult a day, an accumulated assault on the self. Let's say that as a child, you wanted a warm fuzzy from your father every day, but received a cold prickly instead. The cold pricklies and your reaction to them build up like a coral reef. (See Model 5.5 on Page 88.)

The Coral Reef: Barrier Negative Ground

Internally, you have an experience which needs completion. At the same time, you have an equal and opposite force pushing the experience down, out of your awareness. Behind the barrier is your negative ground-of-being decision—perhaps that you're unlovable. Trapped or unexpressed emotions such as fear, hurt, or anger may be part of your barrier as well. Soon, you experience an intrapsychic conflict in that your body wants to complete the experience, while your mind promotes denial and avoidance of the same experience.

MODEL 5.5
**UNEXPERIENCED EXPERIENCE REPRESSED BEHIND
DEFENSE MECHANISMS, EGO IDEAL, AND ACT**

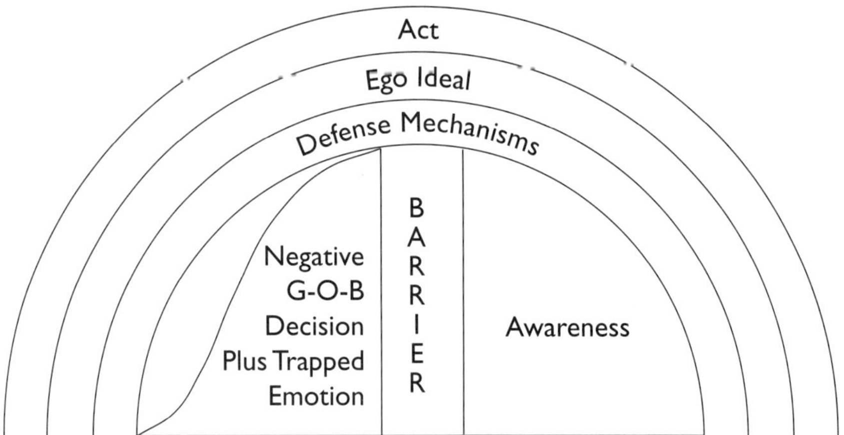

Defense Mechanism: Create the Ego Ideal

Your mind pushes the experience from your awareness and into your unconsciousness. Then, your mind's defense mechanisms take over; you project, rationalize, retroflect, and introject your experience in order to stay unaware of it. You further deny the experience through your ego ideal—your belief in the fantasy world created by your ego.

Look at what you fear and at what you want. If you dream of being rich and powerful, you probably felt powerless and poor as a child. I don't mean poor financially, but poor in the sense of being emotionally impoverished. You experienced a scarcity of touch or connectedness with your mother and father. More than anything, a child longs for the experience of being connected. Lacking that, the child has a negative experience of himself and others; he blocks his bodily experience and moves into the mind and ego experience.

While you suppress your experience, the fantasy you've used to deny the experience seeks simultaneously to be expressed. While you fantasize about being rich and powerful, your negative ground-of-being decision insists that you are powerless. Your organism will attempt to express both decisions. So, you aim to be rich and powerful; but since you really believe you are powerless, you never achieve your goal. No matter how much money you acquire, you still feel poor, because it is never quite enough.

Your Act

Eventually, you project your ego ideal into a conscious manifestation called your *act*. Your act is your public fantasy, the communal illusion about who you are. Your act, by definition, is you not being you. You choose not to be you, because being you doesn't feel good. The bad feeling associated with your experience of yourself originates in your negative ground-of-being, which is based on your inability to meet your parents' expectations. So, through your ego ideal and its projec-

---

Ego ideal vs. negative ground-of-being

    P: How is your ego ideal related to your negative ground-of-being?

Tony: If you remain unclear about your negative ground-of-being, look at your fantasies. Remember your childhood fantasies and dreams because they foreshadowed the serious issues you face now as an adult. Did you ever dream you would fall in love and live happily ever after? The Cinderella fantasy is common to our culture. You know, Cinderella lives a life of misery, waiting for the magical prince to find her and take her away from it all. The fantasy offers more comfort and pleasure than the world of experience.

---

tion, you suppress what you fantasize to be true—your negative ground-of-being which is "I am powerless"—at the same time, you seek desperately to express the fantasy "I am powerful" through your act.

Even when the child's parents are aware and give the child most of what he or she needs, the child will still produce an ego ideal—but it won't be as neurotic or autistic. The child trapped in ego operates outside of reality or experience. (See Model 5.4 on page 87.)

The Normal Neurotic

As an adult, the autistic child uses a very angry, manipulative act to cover up extreme fear. Most of us have a more balanced profile; as normal neurotics, we spend equal time in ego and in experience. (See Model 5.6.)

MODEL 5.6   NORMAL NEUROTIC

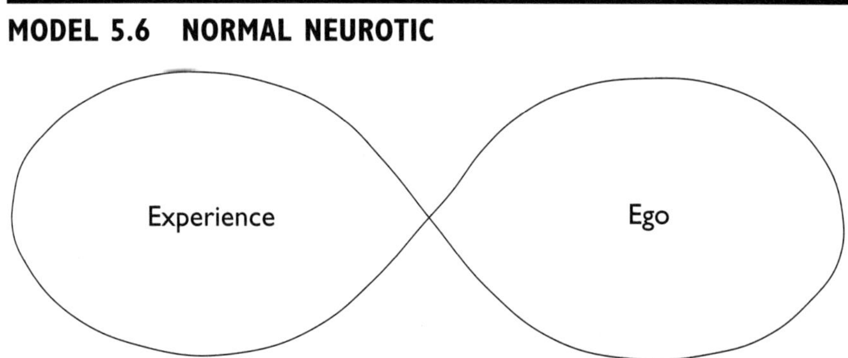

The neurotic is normal in a society which discounts the body and experience, and affirms the mind and the concept. Even the tension and anxiety caused by unexperienced experiences seem normal, even comfortable over time.

Initially, you felt the tension, the holding that resulted from the conflict between reality and ego. For example, as a child, you impulsively wanted to express your anger. But whenever you did, your parents and teachers punished or isolated you. Now, as an adult, whenever your anger surfaces, you tighten up, you push it back down, literally tensing your whole body. Once, the constricted muscles ached, but after a while you no longer noticed.

To illustrate, apply pressure on your arm with your fingers. If you maintain the pressure for fifteen or twenty minutes, you gradually will lose your awareness of the pressure; the pressure becomes normal.

The Mind Shapes the Body Barriers

Ultimately, you shape your body to confirm to your unexperienced experiences. Studies show that your consciousness directly influences your physiological functioning. In other words, if you're mentally upset, you disturb a bodily function; you create physical upset. Certain mind sets, states of consciousness, lead to specific diseases. A certain consciousness triggers cancer, while another leads to cardiovascular problems.

In fact, your frame of mind, your barriers to experience, can suppress your immune system. Consider that we live in a sea of carcinogens, and yet, some people contract cancer, while others don't.

Any change in functioning eventually produces a change in structure. A constant worrier eventually alters the function of his stomach. The more he worries, the more acid his stomach pumps. Soon, the mental upset and the physical change in the form of increased acid lead to a structural change—in this case, an ulcer.

The interaction within and without is complex. But we know that the mind-body split is destructive; as long as we remain unaware of our internal processes, we can kill ourselves without even knowing it.

Barriers

So, your barriers to experience manifest themselves physically. A barrier blocks the flow of information, the flow of awareness, through your universe and your body. In addition, the barrier includes a mental state—generally rationalization or justification—which blocks emotions as well.

Body Blocks

Body blocks manifest in different areas of the body depending on what it is we try to block out. The body block brought on by emotional trauma may be compared to a block caused by physical trauma. For example, in the case of a broken leg, the muscles around the break constrict and lock up. The physical block is your body's response to physical trauma, while the emotional trauma locked in the body is your ego's response to perceived threat.

How do you know when you have a body block? You'll recognize it when an area feels numb or painful when you press on it.

Ocular Block

You can shape your body through a denial of your experience in any or all of seven areas. The ocular block involves the frown muscles between the eyes; these muscles go all the way back to form the skull cap. You

---

Holding it in isn't really healthy

P: Aren't we conditioned to hold in our stomachs? I mean women used to wear girdles and, even without them, we automatically hold in our stomachs.

Tony: That's right, because our culture says, erroneously, that you should have a flat stomach. Our cultural taping process brainwashes women into believing they must fit the form that appeals to men.

P: You know, all my life, I was told to hold in my stomach. And only recently did I realize that it's hard to breathe when you're holding in your stomach.

Tony: You've been conditioned culturally to think there's something wrong with you—that you're overweight—if your stomach sticks out. Have you ever noticed a baby's stomach? Do you know any babies with flat tummies? Absolutely not, because it's not natural.

Remember that movement is a component of aliveness. So the way you hold yourself, the way you carry yourself, determines your degree of aliveness. It's hard to move gracefully when you have to hold in a part of you that normally sticks out, and when you can't take a decent breath.

---

block here when you don't want to be aware of something coming to the surface, such as tears or anger. You contain the flow of emotion by locking up the muscles in the ocular area. And, instead of the emotion, you experience a headache.

Oral Block

If you grind your teeth or lock your jaw, consider that you are holding or biting back. The oral block constricts self-expression. Remember when your mother said, "Don't ever say that again"? The person with an oral block stifles self-expression to please others. The process of building the block begins when you activate the energy of the experience and stifle yourself. You encounter your ego ideal which leads you to your act, which is to please someone else.

Throat Block

You also can block in the throat area. You can choke it down, swallow it down. If you choke during conscious breathing, think about what you're choking on. When you have an oral block, you bite down; with a throat block you tighten the muscles in your neck. For example, when you feel tears come to the surface, if you have a throat block, your neck and jaw begin to ache in your effort to deny the tears.

Chest Block

When you block in the chest area, you constrict a group of muscles called the intracostals, which start at the sternum and go around to the spine. A block in this area often leads to cardiovascular problems. If you hold tension in your diaphragm, you create a diaphragmatic block which may manifest as respiratory illness.

Abdominal Block

If you block in the abdominal region, in the gastrointestinal tract, you end up with ulcers, gastroenteritis, and colitis. Generally, you hold onto fear in the abdominal area. You tighten up your stomach when you are afraid in order to block awareness of the fear.

Pelvic Block

The last block can occur in the pelvic girdle. Blocking in this area eliminates another component of aliveness: your sexuality. Historically, the pelvic area functions as the seat of powerful emotions such as anger and rage. Remember that as children we were what Freud called polymorphously perverse. That is, poly meaning "many" and morphous meaning "shapes"; a child's body then moves like the Pillsbury dough boy's. As adults, if we could eliminate barriers and blocks in the pelvic area, we too could experience our sexuality and our emotions directly, powerfully, and completely.

Healing the Mind-Body Split: Re-own Your Experience

What can you do to become whole and complete? How can you heal the mind-body split? You have to re-own your experience; you have to go back, be willing to allow yourself to experience those things you did not allow yourself to experience before.

Breathe

Breathing is one way to begin to take back your experiences. As you relax and breathe consciously, you will become aware of tension in your body; you will be forced to recognize directly your body blocks, the barriers you erected within your body.

Body Work

Body work—bioenergetics, breathing, rebirthing—helps you locate your particular body blocks and so you can begin to release the barriers. As you breathe deeply and consciously, you will increase the charge in your body and the energy will run into the barriers or body blocks. You will become aware then of the blocks, experience where you close down, where you deny. You can have a direct experience of your ego acting through your body, controlling, limiting your experience. Stay conscious of it.

Know that whatever starts kicking, whatever demands your attention, as you do the breathing—that's your unexperienced experience, the hidden treasure waiting for you behind the barrier. That's what you've been hoarding for a lifetime. If you stay with it and continue the breathing, you can move through the barrier. You can open the treasure chest and find awareness, the map which can lead you back to your birthright: aliveness.

Life

Your actions are the dance of life
Your feelings are the music
So
Dance to the music

We Are What We Suppress . . . We Are What We Express

The shape of your body reveals the record of what you suppressed, what you inhibited, and what you expressed, as you grew up. In combination with other factors, including body tissue, brain activity, metabolism, and reaction to gravity, your response to events and people formed your body type. Your body structure, as a foundation for influencing your behavior, led to the formation of your character type.

What Kind of Body Do You Have? It's Up to Your Tissue

Three types of tissue combine to form our bodies: visceratonia, somatonia, cerebratonia. According to Alexander Lowen, the proportion of each type of tissue determines the basic body types: endomorph, mesomorph, ectomorph.

- ◆ **Endomorph.** The endomorphic body contains mostly visceral or gut tissue, found in the digestive and eliminative systems. The body tends to be physically plump, with rounded rather than angular musculature. The endomorph, when stressed, needs other people and chooses to turn to them for support.

- **Mesomorph.** The mesomorphic body consists mostly of somatic or muscular tissue. The mesomorph has well developed muscles and bones. Often, the body type resembles a wedge of cheese stuck on two toothpicks; in other words, the upper half has been well developed. Mesomorphs like action, and, when under stress, meet the challenge alone.

- **Ectomorph.** The predominance of the third type of tissue, cerebrotonia, leads to the ectomorphic body type. Ectomorphs have well developed nervous systems. They enjoy solitude and tend to retreat into their minds.

So, our genetic composition partially determines how we receive and express the energy available to us. However, our interactions with the environment—especially with our parents—reinforces innate behavior patterns. The combination of our genetic disposition with external factors leads to formation of our temperament.

What Determines Your Temperament

The expression of our temperament occurs within the three parts of the brain: the brain stem, which influences activity and movement; the instinctual or the emotional brain, which surrounds the brain stem, and includes survival tapes; and the cerebral cortex, the outer part of the brain which controls or inhibits the activity of both the instinctual brain and the activity brain.

Cortical Control

Whether you exhibit high or low cortical control depends on the degree of inhibition by the cortex on the instinctual and activity brains.

- **High cortical control.** If you have high cortical control, you tend to be logical, to analyze, and to withdraw from contact with people and external reality. You inhibit and suppress your emotions as well as your actions. The ectomorph, with his tendency to think and analyze, exhibits high cortical control. He tends to inhibit emotional expression.

◆ **Low cortical control.** If your cortical control is low, you tend to be more dynamic. The undercontrolled person demonstrates high emotional and physical activity. He tends to be very emotional or very action-oriented, as illustrated by the mesomorph. In the undercontrolled person, the instinctual brain predominates.

Autonomic Nervous System

In addition to the cortex, the autonomic nervous system also influences your activity level and your behavior through regulation of your metabolism. As with cortical control, either one of two aspects can predominate: the para-sympathetic or the sympathetic.

◆ **Para-sympathetic.** The para-sympathetic aspect calms you down and keeps you relaxed. It deactivates your stress by slowing down your heart beat and your metabolic rate. The para-sympathetic personality tends to be more intuitive and tries to figure things out.

◆ **Sympathetic.** The sympathetic nervous system activates you and prepares you to respond to stress and to change. The sympathetically oriented type tends to be a mesomorph—very action-oriented.

Gravity Mechanism

One other factor contributes to formation of character type. How you respond to gravity, the force that pulls you down and keeps you grounded, determines how centered you will be. To refer to someone as well grounded implies that he has his feet firmly planted on the ground.

Developmental Stages and Character Type

The combination of these factors—your relationship with gravity, your metabolism, and your brain activity— along with your unique reaction to trauma or stress at a particular stage in your development determine your character type. Ron Kurtz, in *The Body Reveals,* outlines the character types as they emerge during four developmental stages: tactile, oral, anal, and genital.

The trauma and your reaction to it may lead to two possible character types within each developmental stage. For example, if you experienced trauma in the tactile stage, your character type may be Schizophrenic or Schizoid. At the oral level, you could be Oral or Psychopath 1. In the anal stage, your character type may be labeled Psychopath 2 or Masochist. And, at the genital stage, you may show Hysteric or Phallic character tendencies.

Tactile Stage

The tactile stage includes the developmental period from birth until age one or two. A disturbance in the mother-child contact during the tactile stage, especially if the mother physically and emotionally rejects the child, produces either the Schizophrenic or the Schizoid types.

Schizophrenic

The Schizophrenic exhibits low cortical control. The Schizophrenic tends to express a high level of dynamic, emotional activity, which generally is directed internally. There is an extreme withdrawal from external reality and active creation of an inner reality composed of voices (delusions) and visions (hallucinations).

The fundamental conflict of the Schizophrenic is existence vs. nonexistence. He believes that to survive he must split off from external reality and create a defensive internal reality. This splitting of awareness produces an over-active mind and an under-active body. Thus, his perception and relationship with gravity is "top heavy" and "bottom light," with a consequent diminished awareness of body sensations and expanded and amplified awareness of verbal and visual expression.

Schizoid

The Schizoid has high cortical control. The Schizoid or, in layman's terms, the Sensitive/Analytic, is a more common character type.

In the tactile stage, the child makes no distinction between himself and the world; he believes he and the world are one. The child never gains the ability to distinguish between himself and his mother. Generally, the Schizoid dissociates himself from his feelings; he never coordinates his thinking and feeling. Because the disturbance occurs at the fundamental level of touch, the child withdraws from the world, from experience—even from contact with his own body—and thus, reinforces a diminished sense of self. As an adult, he avoids intimate relationships.

Influenced by the sympathetic nervous system and high cortical control, the body is thin and tight, and moves energetically, but stiffly. The head often seems disconnected from the body, which again splits at the waist.

The Schizoid's basic life issue can be stated as "Existence vs. Need." The Schizoid says, "I can exist if I don't need closeness. So, in order to survive, I'll withdraw contact and intimacy with others." He often feels uncertain about belonging, so he escapes through withdrawal, thought, and fantasy. He shows sensitivity to overload, interruptions, and emotional closeness. In spite of his great need, he offers much through his ability to theorize, analyze, and imagine.

"I feel confused," summarizes the Schizoid's TA (Transactional Analysis) program. On the TA sweatshirt, you find the obvious message on the front: "If I reach out, I'll die"; on the back, you read the hidden message which is "Stay away—I'm afraid." The Schizoid script originates in the mother's rejection and terrorization of the child through her own internal crazy child. The child splits and becomes autistic in order to survive.

Some of the irrational beliefs based on the Schizoid's negative ground-of-being include: "I can't coordinate my feelings and thoughts." "If I reach out, I'll be hurt." "I have to give up my need to be close to survive." Common injunctions are "don't feel; don't trust; don't be sane." The Schizoid assumes the "be strong; be perfect" counterscript. He plays the following games: Blemish, NIGYSOB, Kick Me. Distraction, withdrawal, and anger make up the Schizoid common rackets.

What is a counterscript?

P: What is a counterscript?

Tony: The counterscript is the compensation or the act. It's what you do to avoid being aware of your negative ground-of-being; it is the opposite of your script.

Oral Stage

A disruption in development in the oral stage can lead to the Oral character type (low cortical control) or to the Psychopath 1 type (high cortical control). The para-sympathetic nervous system influences both types.

In the oral stage, the child needs to feel supported, loved, nurtured. During this stage, he differentiates between himself and mother, between himself and other people. This stage begins around age two.

Now, the Schizoid child knows his mother doesn't want him; she never holds him or cares for him on a basic, physical level. In the oral stage, the child receives some support, but not enough. He decides, "If I am independent, I must give up needing support and warmth. I can express my need as long as I'm not independent." The basic issue is "Need vs. Dependence." Because he did not receive enough contact as a child, he experiences the world as unnurturing and unsupportive.

Oral or Dependent/Enduring

The Dependent/Enduring personality, the layman's term for the Oral type, feels very needy, as if he will never be filled up. The thin, long, ectomorphic body reflects this need. He lacks energy and strength, especially in the lower half of the body. The underdeveloped musculature creates undercharging in the arms and legs. He breathes shallowly and cuts off his respiration to deaden his feelings.

Generally, as an infant, he felt dependent and unfulfilled. The frustration led to clinging and inner need for support. Primarily, he experienced deprivation of love. As an adult, he cannot be alone because he feels empty and depressed.

Compensated Oral or Self-Reliant

Sometimes, the Compensated Oral evolves from the Dependent/ Enduring counterscript. The Compensated Oral or Self-Reliant type feels uncertain about external support. He braces for challenges, likes to do it himself, and as a result, has problems depending on others. On the other hand, the Dependent/Enduring type tends to give up under pressure, because he lacks faith in his ability to contribute; he needs too much himself. "I feel helpless," sums up the TA program for both the Dependent/Enduring and the Self-Reliant types. The front of the TA sweatshirt reads: "Please fill me up," while the back says, "Nobody ever does."

The Oral script emanates from a loss or continued absence of the mother, in addition to angry feelings about rejection by the father. The child irrationally believes that he can't make it on his own, but that reaching out leads to rejection. So he assumes exaggerated strength and stubborn independence (Self-Reliant) as a counterscript. The Self-Reliant type decides early that his need will not be met; so he decides to do it himself, and sacrifices warmth and available support for rigid independence.

Oral types play the following games: Poor Me, If It Weren't For You, Self-Blemish, Addict, Kick Me. Favorite rackets include depression and inadequacy.

Psychopath 1 or Tough/Generous

The second possible typology within the oral stage is the Psychopath. Actually, the Psychopathic typology is transitional between the oral and anal stages. So, you find the Psychopath 1 (Tough/Generous) in the oral stage, and the Psychopath 2 (Charming/Seductive) in the anal stage.

Generally, the Psychopath has a large, inflated body. He tends to be top heavy, with the pelvis undercharged. The Tough/Generous type has a rigid body, in contrast to the more supple and attractive body of the Charming/Seductive type. In both cases, the eyes are watchful and distrustful, a trait which leads to ocular blocks as well as to emotional blocks related to seeing and understanding.

The basic issue for the Psychopath revolves around "Independence vs. Closeness," which can be expressed as "You can be close to me, as long as I can control you." Generally, the Psychopath denies feelings and opts for the mind and ego. The Tough/Generous profile begins with a controlling and domineering mother figure; the Charming/ Seductive profile originates in parental seduction which involves sexual or emotional manipulation.

The Psychopath has a strong need for control and a drive for power, which he acquires either through bullying (Tough/Generous) or through seduction (Charming/Seductive). He enjoys making others dependent on him so he does not have to express his own need.

The Tough/Generous type fears he cannot hold his own. He's sensitive to being used or humiliated. In relationships, he has trouble being equal and open with others. The Charming/Seductive type feels insecure about interference with his needs. He tends to seduce, charm, and manipulate. He has trouble feeling satisfied, feeling his needs are met. In relationships, he manipulates others as a way to handle the frustration of having to deal with them.

The TA program describes the psychopathic type as someone who enjoys making fools of others. The sweatshirt reads: "Love Me" on the front, with "Or I'll Kill You" on the back. The script evolves out of the child's decision to control the parent through seduction. He learns that he can control by making others need him. Because he fears manipulation, he seduces others into needing him; only then, do his own needs surface.

The script includes the following injunctions: "Don't feel. Don't be you. Don't trust. Don't be a child." Counterscript injunctions are: "Be strong; try hard; please me." Psychopaths like to play games such as Cops and Robbers, Kick Me, NIGYSOB, Corner, Uproar, Buzz Off, and Blemish. Thinking instead of feeling, confusion, and bravado are common rackets of the Psychopath.

Anal Stage

To clarify the Psychopath 2 profile, let's look at the general characteristics of the anal stage. In the anal stage, the infant receives enough support to successfully handle life issues. In the anal stage, the child realizes he has an impact on the world, and he begins to assert that. So the issue at the anal level involves discovery and use of power and control. The child realizes he can manipulate Mom into getting what he wants or by not doing what she wants him to do.

Masochist or Burdened/Enduring

The second aspect of the anal state is the Masochist. The Burdened/

Enduring type has a short, thick, muscular body. Although the body is fully charged, he holds it tightly, choking off energy at the neck and waist.

"Closeness vs. Freedom" is the Masochist's basic issue. "If I'm free, you won't love me; so I'll be good and then, you'll love me." Because he can't be good and because he is not loved for being himself, the Masochist feels very angry. He complains, suffers, and whines, but remains passive. So, while the Masochist pleases others, he feels much anger and resentment on the inside. At some point, the suppressed negativity has to be expressed, so he provokes volatile behavior in other people to justify his own, inevitable explosion.

He feels uncertain about the effect of his actions on others and, in relationships, he becomes easily frustrated with others' mistakes and irresponsibility. The Masochist dislikes being hurried or pushed. He enjoys taking on responsibility; and his major strengths include loyalty, endurance, and permanence.

"I'll be a good boy or girl," sums up the Masochist's TA program. The sweatshirt reads: "I'm really trying" on the front and "I'm mad as hell" on the back. Typically, the child receives love and acceptance in combination with severe pressure. The parent crushes any resistance, which makes the child feel trapped. Masochists have a strong fear of being cut off. The child adopts a passive, submissive attitude—the Adaptive Child—in order to get parental strokes. However, beneath the suffering veneer lie the angry feelings of the Vengeful Child. The Adapted Child feels guilty about assertive behavior; as an adult, he stays trapped through his own self-defeating behaviors.

Injunctions include "don't be assertive; don't think; don't enjoy; don't have needs; don't be weak." Injunctions such as "please me; try hard; be perfect" form the counterscript.

The Masochist plays games such as Stupid, Sunny Side Up, Uproar, NIGYSOB, Kick Me, Harried, Why Does This Always Happen To Me, Look How Hard I'm Trying. The Masochist loves to play the angry victim, to suffer from a martyr position.

Genital Stage

In the fourth stage, the genital, you find two types: Phallic or Industrious/Overfocused and Hysteric or Expressive/Clinging. Generally, genital types rigidly defend because they fear giving in and being used by others. They have strong egos and enjoy competition.

The body type looks integrated and has a good flow of energy in the peripheral points. Still, the body is somewhat rigid during movement. The Phallic type has a more athletic body than the Hysteric who has a more sensual body type.

Phallic or Industrious/Overfocused

The basic issue is "Freedom vs. Surrender to Love." The genital type believes he can be free as long as he doesn't lose his head, so he holds back impulses to reach out. While he has a strong ego and good reality contact, he keeps himself contained. The Hysteric eventually expresses the excess build up of energy in a melodramatic way. The Industrious/ Overfocused, or the Phallic, holds onto the energy and tends to become rigid and quietly self-righteous.

The Industrious/Overfocused feels insecure about his worth and other's appreciation of it. To compensate, he spends most of his time working. Thus, in relationships, he is too busy for others who then experience him as cold and impersonal. The Phallic type becomes easily frustrated by delays, worries about his performance, and yearns for equality. His attributes include productivity, persistence, and loyalty.

Hysteric or Expressive/Clinging

The Hysteric has trouble believing that others are sincerely interested in him. The father influences the child's development at this stage. Originally, the child had a warm and loving relationship with the father, especially if the child was a girl. But when the daughter reaches puberty, the father withdraws because he feels threatened by his sexual feelings for his daughter. The daughter feels rejected and confused and then tries to get his attention again in any way that she can. So, the Hysteric fears rejection, especially in the sense of not being heard or understood. So, in relationships he needs attention and wants to be liked and understood. While he tends to exaggerate feelings, his high energy and enthusiasm attracts others.

The TA program can be stated as: "I won't give in." The sweatshirt reads: "I'm Available" on the front and "Buzz Off" on the back. Genital types tend to be stiff and fear giving in because they equate it with submission. They tend to play Wooden Leg, which involves taking an imagined inferiority, imperfection, or physical problem and using it as a justification to feel like a loser.

Injunctions include "don't think; don't grow; don't feel what you feel." Genital types assume injunctions such as "please me; try hard; be strong; look good" as their counterscripts. So while they really want love, they are too scared to ask for it. Games include Rapo, Courtroom, NIGYSOB, and Wooden Leg, with an emphasis on covering up feelings of suffering and inadequacy.

Summary: Developmental Stages

To summarize, at the tactile level you deal with your existence. At the oral level, you cope with feeling supported and belonging. At the anal level, you work with control and power. And at the genital level, you handle relationships with self and others.

The mother primarily influences the child's movement or dormancy in the first two developmental stages. The father has more influence on the child in the last two developmental stages.

If you have a severe trauma at any of these stages in your development, then you are stuck there. As an adult, you deal now with the unresolved issues characteristic of that developmental stage. In the oral stage, you have issues around being needy, around being loved and belonging. If you find yourself in either of the Psychopath positions, you have issues around control and power. And if you have issues related to the genital stage, you need to work on your relationships.

The sympathetic nervous system is primarily active for both of the tactile and genital stages. So the sympathetic system is overactive in the Schizoid, Schizophrenic, Hysteric, and Phallic character types. The para-sympathetic stage is active in the oral and anal stages.

Realize too that unexperienced experiences at any level also alter your relationship to gravity. If you feel that you are up in the air, your trauma occurred in either of the first two developmental stages. So, the Schizoid, the Psychopath 1, and the Schizophrenic tend to displace the energy that was evenly distributed at birth upward into their minds.

You find overgrounding in the last two developmental stages. The Psychopath 2, the Masochist, the Hysteric, and the Phallic tend to feel weighted down, to feel burdened. The Masochist or the Burdened/Enduring especially illustrates this: They look and act as if they have a heavy weight on their shoulders. The Industrious/Overfocused also is very responsible and rigid.

If you want to determine where you fit in, take your craziness as an adult and intensify it. Notice how you react when stressed, pressured, or rejected. Your typical reaction will place you within the stages. Don't rely primarily on your body type to determine your developmental stage. Body type is only a part of character type, and it can aid you in understanding and working with an unexperienced experience at any

---

Other questions about developmental stages

P: Do some people escape all four of these stages?

Tony: It would be difficult to move through all four stages without experiencing trauma at some point. But if you can get through the first three, you have a strong developmental foundation.

P: How can two brothers end up being so different? My brother and I had the same parents and were born only two years apart. And yet, we are so different.

Tony: Your difference depends on the way each of you choose to organize your experience of growing up at each developmental stage. Also, your parents responded differently to each of you, although it may not seem that way to you.

P: If you get stuck in the oral stage, does that mean you stay there for the rest of your life?

Tony: You may or you may not. Let's say you didn't feel supported in the oral stage, so you have some unexperienced experiences around people not taking care of you. As a child, you may not have been able to handle those issues. Still, it is possible to cope with the trauma over time. Your present body structure and behavioral patterns do not necessarily condemn you to life imprisonment in a certain developmental stage.

---

level. But your body may not match exactly the character type to which you belong.

Actually, no one is a pure Schizoid or pure Hysteric or pure Psychopath. As you move through the developmental stages, you experience a series of traumas within each stage. Your primary character type depends on your unique life experiences and on how you handled or mishandled the issues at that stage.

Don't Take It Personally

Remember not to take any of this personally. It's important to realize that you can change your character type; you can change any of it at any point. You have to be willing to handle the issues of the stage you're stuck in, which means you find the best way to experience out the feelings around the issue. You can break out of the closed loop process and move on. You can handle it now, from a new position of awareness and mastery.

Relationships

*S/he who wants the most in a relationship gets
the least*
*S/he who wants the least in a relationship gets
the most*
*S/he who wants everything in a relationship
gets nothing*
*S/he who wants nothing in a relationship gets
everything*
*So to get the most in your relationship, want
the least*
*And to get everything in your relationship,
want nothing*

Riding the Roller Coaster of Involvement

In the beginning of what most of us label a relationship, we feel great. We love our partner, and life seems exhilarating. The prospect of spending a lifetime with another human being is nothing less than wondrous. In fact, the thrill, in the beginning, feels much like the excitement of riding a roller coaster up to the top, edging toward the brink of a vast, new world.

But then, as you travel further in the relationship, the descent into hell begins. The first time we encounter the other person's craziness, the first time they, or worse, we, fall off the pedestal, we plummet unwillingly and unconsciously into reality.

Why do so many of our relationships begin so positively and end so badly? Actually, what most people call relationships are not relationships at all. They are better described as *entanglements* and *involvements*.

Involvement

What is an involvement and how does it differ from a relationship? According to Werner Erhard, involve means "to make intricate, tangled, or complicated; to entangle in difficulty, trouble or danger." If your relationship seems complicated, it is not really a relationship; it is an involvement. An involvement also implies "drawing or holding within itself." So, if you use your relationship as a retreat, as a way to hide or withdraw from the world, it is not a relationship; it is an involvement.

Involve also means "to include by necessity; to require." Someone who needs to be in relationship believes the following: "If I'm in a relationship with you—great; I'm happy; life is wonderful. But if you leave, or if the relationship changes, my life is over; I'm in pain." If that's the way you feel in your present relationship, you actually are involved in an involvement.

Involve also means "to make busy, employ, occupy." If you are marking time or filling up the hours, you are not in a relationship. You are in an involvement.

The Illusion of Loneliness

We fear loneliness almost as much as the threat of disease. More than five billion people live on this planet. How can we be alone? We perceive ourselves as lonely for two reasons: We don't like ourselves, and we don't like anyone else; no one, including ourselves, meets our personal checklist or expectations.

Since few people meet the requirements, we eliminate the possibility of relationships with a number of people. Some people follow their checklist so closely that no one fits the requirements, and they end up being alone, as feared.

Most of us choose involvements and entanglements because we don't know how to create a real relationship. Anything, it seems, is better than the prospect of being lonely and alone.

Loneliness as Separation Anxiety

With all the available people in the world, loneliness is an illusion and is self-imposed. The state of loneliness actually indicates a separation within the self; it is a splitting off of the awareness of yourself as well as awareness of the universe. Loneliness as an alienation from the self does lead to estrangement from others. We do not connect with the aware self within; we do not listen to our hearts, so it follows that we fail to connect, heart to heart, with others. We do not relate; instead, out of desperation, we settle for involvements and entanglements.

Entanglements

Dictionaries define entangle as "to involve in or catch, as in a net." So, if you experience frustration in your relationship, call it an entanglement. In contrast, a relationship is effortless. An entanglement also implies mental confusion. So, if you find yourself struggling to make the relationship work, but feel confused about how to do that, you are in an entanglement.

Relationship Allows for Periodical Craziness

Does that mean you never have to work at making a relationship better? Do you never experience your own or the other person's craziness when you're in a relationship?

Within the relationship, you do experience times of involvement and entanglement. But the craziness surfaces periodically rather than chronically. The relationship and the people in it can allow for occasional feelings of inadequacy and confusion. Each person can allow for craziness because each person possesses a sense of self and others as whole, complete, and perfect.

In a relationship, you *allow for* each other's games; you expect games to surface and, when they do, you don't take them personally. In a relationship, you create a safe space for all that it means to be human. You allow for the games, the craziness, *but you don't feed or add to it.*

Over time, in a real relationship, the craziness decreases as the couple learns to harmonize and balance. They listen to each other, and their love and their caring permeate their interaction. That's not to say that she never nags and he never withdraws. It means that they don't create those times as the center of their relationship.

You see, relationships are extremely rare. There are probably as many people in relationships as there are people who are celibate. The creative management of a relationship has several requirements, none of which will be on your checklist.

First, you must have a successful relationship with yourself. Establishing satisfying relationships can only occur after you've mastered yourself, which means you have handled your machinery.

If you've managed yourself, your chances for establishing a real relationship increase. You are less likely to take personally the other person's games; you are more likely to focus on reality. You know your purpose and what you want in the relationship. Most important, you give up your belief that you are separate and know that you are part of the whole.

Universal Experience

Imagine that the universe is a large box. (See Model 7.1.) If you place yourself within the box, universal experience becomes available to you.

Within the circle of yourself, you exist complete and whole. You know that you are okay alone, by yourself. If you know that to be true, then you are able and willing to expand your awareness; you assume responsibility for being the source of your own experience. When you can do that, you also can augment your sense of self to include another person. You realize being in a relationship can enhance your life so that you experience yourself directly as well as indirectly through the eyes of another person. Consider how much more you have to experience; your whole universe has expanded.

Only then, does the illusion of being separate disappear. Being a part of everything, you never encounter the myth of loneliness again. Loneliness, entanglement, and involvement are all illusions; contact, connectedness, and relationship are realities.

You traded in the truth for the lie soon after birth. In the womb, your mother met all your needs. And you felt happy, comfortable. You experienced love directly and completely. But at birth, you experienced physical and emotional separation from your source, your mother. Soon after came your awareness that, to some extent, you were on your own.

As you grew, you experienced many times the realization that you depended on your parents for survival. You realized too that not all of your needs would be met. Out of your struggle to survive and your fear that you wouldn't make it, you forgot the basic nature of the universe— harmonious connection and all-one-ness. And so, you spend the remainder of your life trying to grapple with the fear that you are separate and alone.

MODEL 7.1   UNIVERSAL EXPERIENCE

The Universe

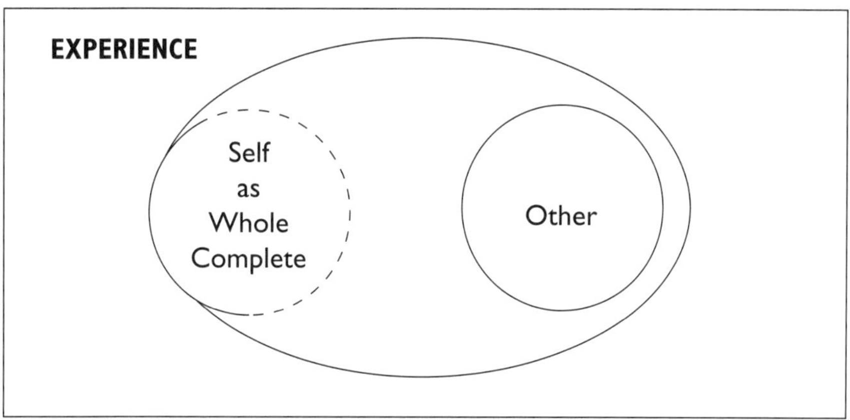

Stage 1: No Fun

As an adult, you set up a pattern which verifies and assures your loneliness and unhappiness. (See Model 7.2 on page 117.) You sit at home in a state of misery that Stewart Emery calls *No Fun*. And really, it isn't any fun. You've created your life so that you are alone and lonely. In pain, you decide to venture out, with your checklist in hand, to find somebody or something to make life okay for you. Then, when you find the right person, you finally can be happy, finally be fulfilled.

It's as if you're living out a movie scene in which you've barricaded yourself behind fort walls waiting for Indians to attack at any moment, while secretly hoping that John Wayne and the cavalry will save you.

Stage 2: Falling in Love

In the second stage, you *Fall in Love*. There's good news and bad news about the second stage. The bad news is John Wayne isn't coming; the knight in shining armor doesn't exist; Sleeping Beauty won't appear.

The good news is that there aren't any Indians either. You are not under siege; you are your own enemy. But, in your unawareness, you don't know about the good news yet.

When you fall in love, you achieve a state Stewart Emery called "temporary well-being." You feel euphoric, because you believe you've found someone who meets your checklist; you base your love on form, a taped list of what and who you need to be happy. You know you've become a form junkie when the mad, passionate, ecstatic feelings associated with love consume you.

Life seems wonderful again, but your hope and reliance on someone else to make you happy, eventually imprisons you. Falling in love turns your life into a runaway emotional roller coaster. You alternate between joy over your discovery of a new love and the fear that your love will end or disappear.

Still, the good feelings feel so good that they overshadow our fear and inspire us to try to capture the other person. Many of us marry and make promises to love forever until death do us part. But then, when the other person falls off the pedestal, when they no longer fit the form, we begin to start praying for the "'til death do us part" part. When we realize our mate is only human after all, we fall out of love. Actually we never loved the person; we loved the form.

When you *fall* in love, you are willing to love only the good. When you *be* in love, you recognize the person as a human being and you allow for both the good and bad in the relationship.

Stage 3: Doubt and Confusion

Falling out of love with the form leads to the third stage: *Doubt and Confusion*. Because you lack the training needed to identify, create, and maintain a genuine relationship, the detour into reality seems overwhelming. Instead, you model your relationship after your parents' relationship and rely upon the training you received from them. In short, you use coercion and manipulation to put the relationship back on track.

You let yourself fall into the if-you-really-loved-me-you-would trap. *I love you* are the three most manipulative words in the language.

MODEL 7.2   ILLUSION OF SEPARATENESS

Stage 1: NO FUN

Stage 2: FALLING IN LOVE
  "Temporary Well-Being"

Stage 3: DOUBT AND CONFUSION

Stage 4: DESPAIR AND DISILLUSIONMENT

Stage 4: Despair and Disillusionment

Still, some people stay in the relationship and struggle to bring it back to the illusion of early romance. If they persist, they descend into the final stage: *Despair and Disillusionment.* Remember that when you fell in love, your partner seemed perfect to you; you experienced the relationship as completely positive. In the final stage, you view the other person as evil and the relationship as totally negative. The roller coaster comes to a halt and the relationship ends in divorce court.

So, after divorce court, where do you find yourself? You return to the No Fun stage. Again, you've created a closed loop pattern. When you return to stage one, you're hurting, so you tend to erect more barriers, more walls to prevent a recurrence of the pattern. The good news is you keep the enemies out; the bad news is you keep yourself locked in.

So why do we keep doing it? Why do some people marry three or four times?

Stage two, falling in love, feeds the pattern. Falling in love feels so good, becomes so addictive, that people continue the search for romance, if only temporary. Also, we don't realize that we can create a genuine relationship, because we are trained to create entanglements.

We never assume responsibility for our own happiness; we become jaded as we see ourselves and the universe as inferior and incomplete.

So, in the last two stages, when we reach doubt and confusion, despair and disillusionment, we project our responsibility onto the partner through blame: "If it weren't for you . . ."

He's/She's the Problem

The following pattern is common in relationship counseling. I usually talk to the wife first. I'll ask her, "Do you know what the problem is?" And she'll say, "Yes. He (her husband) is the problem. You have to fix him. He's gone all the time. And when he finally comes home, he won't talk to me. And I've been with kids all day and I'd like some adult conversation, so I try to get him to talk. But all he wants to do is drink beer and watch TV. And if I push it, he withdraws even more and eventually becomes hostile and angry. You've got to fix him. He's the problem."

So, I say, "Well, send the problem in. I'm wasting my time with you. Let me get to the source of your difficulties."

Enter the problem. I ask him, "What's the problem with your relationship?" He says, "She's the problem; you've got to fix her. I work my fingers to the bone trying to earn a decent living, and when I get home, all she wants to do is talk. I just want a little peace, but no, she sticks to me like mud on a pig. And she stays on me until I have to push her away. You've got to fix her; she's the problem."

In an entanglement, the other person is always the problem. In an entanglement, you harass each other, you pursue each other, and you use each other to hurt yourself. Let me demonstrate: Get into a group of three or four people and sit closely to each other. Then, with your right hand, take hold of the left wrist of the person sitting to your right. Now, make a fist out of your left hand, the one being held by someone else. And then, beat yourself in the face with it.

Good, and now complain bitterly to that person sitting next to you. Go ahead; tell them it's their fault. Use them as an excuse to justify beating yourself. You now have experienced a live demonstration of the dynamics of an entanglement.

As long as you blame the other person, you disown your responsibility. And, as long as you deny responsibility, you are destined to repeat the pattern. Your belief that you are separate feeds the pattern and your continuation of it.

To disconnect the closed loop pattern, you must journey into your awareness. You will have to acknowledge your games, your negative ground-of-being, as well as that of your partner. And then, you will have to include the other person in your universe of awareness and experience. You must be bigger than the games.

As long as you stay locked in the smallness of your negative ground, you experience insufficiency, confusion, and disillusionment. As long as you believe you're separate, you shrink your universe, your experience, and your opportunity for aliveness.

By experiencing yourself as whole and complete, while simultaneously including your negative ground-of-being, you expand your universe. A good relationship with self and with others does not exclude the negative, but includes and allows for it as part of reality.

Give up Your Forms

You also will have to give up your forms, the boundaries you've imposed on yourself, on others, and on your relationships. As you relinquish the old patterns, you'll encounter your training and conditioning, as well as your emotions. The role you've played in past relationships will determine which emotions you'll have to confront.

If you've assumed an Adaptive Child position in your relationships, you will experience guilt when you move out of your traditional role in the pattern. You also will confront your fear, if you define guilt as fear associated with punishment.

If you played the role of Rebellious Child, expect to confront your anger. The Rebel chooses resistance to others as a way to express anger; so when you drop the resistance, when you stop locking into an opposing position in your relationship, you will directly experience your anger.

I/Thou Relationship

In an I/Thou relationship (See Model 7.3 on page 121), you create a direct experience of connectedness; you know we are all the same; we are all part of the universe. And so, you rarely experience isolation and alienation.

When you don't want to be in a relationship

P: Tony, what if you don't want to be in a relationship? I mean I feel good about not being in one. I've been traveling and meeting lots of exciting people, but I don't seem to have a need to bond with them. On the one hand, I feel good about that—about not needing to be in a relationship, but I also feel guilty. I feel that maybe I'm being selfish. Do you think I'm avoiding relationships?

Tony: Move your awareness out of your mind and into your heart. Is your guilt a game created by your mind? I suggest that you simply enjoy yourself. But base your enjoyment on what your heart tells you, rather than what your mind generates.

Earlier this year, I decided to devote my time to and energy to study and work and to take a break from relationships. After awhile though, I began to realize I felt lonely. In fact, staying at home alone is about the worst thing you can do when you've ended a relationship. It's okay not to want intimate involvement with someone, but you don't want to cut yourself off from the world. You can relate without having to be in a romantic relationship.

P: Actually, my guilt comes and goes. I've never married, and I've never really settled down. Although I have had two long-term relationships that lasted a total of ten years, I haven't really been involved with anyone for the past three years. I guess my guilt comes from the feeling that, at my age, I should settle down. And yet I like my life exactly the way it is. I have a good time.

Tony: Let me give you one more definition: recreation. Many people prefer a *recreationship* instead of a relationship. Recreation means to play or refresh oneself with games, pastimes, or amusements. I'm not referring to the negative TA games, but to amusing, relaxing, entertaining games. It's okay to want a recreationship; not everyone needs or wants a relationship. However, many relationships spring from recreationships; a friendship based on recreation can bloom into a future relationship. Look at your own experience and listen to your heart whenever the guilt surfaces.

The other person represents a different piece of the pie, another piece of reality. Your awareness of the universal pie and your own place in it enables you to create a growing and enriched relationship. You then can fully experience your own universe as well as that of the other person. In fact, your experience quadruples as you also gain the experience of the other person's experience of you.

MODEL 7.3   ENTANGLEMENT

PERCEIVED DIFFERENCES

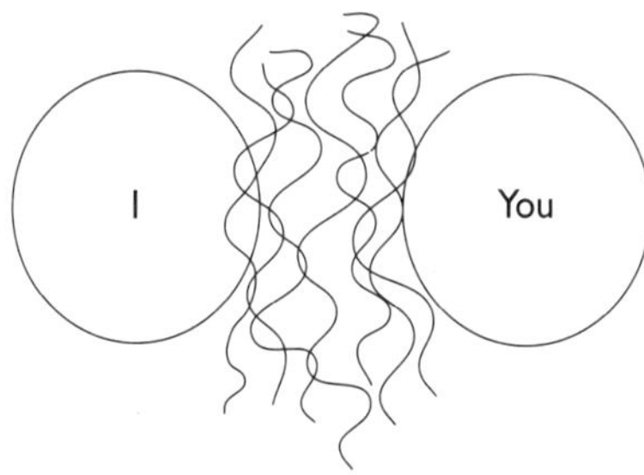

"I/Thou" Relationship

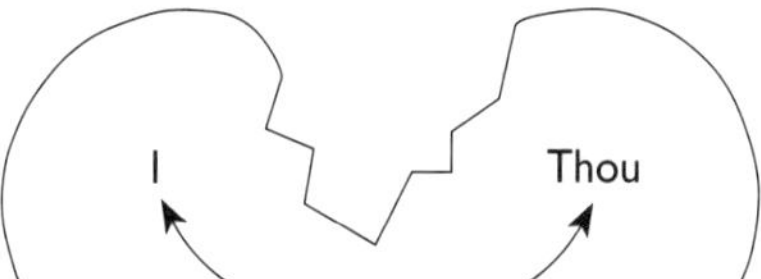

What Is a Relationship?

Werner Erhard defines a relationship as "the quality or state of being related"; it is a connection. Relationship also means "to understand, to be aware of someone else." Relationship, as a condition of being connected, joined, associated, implies sharing through mutual participation. To sum up, a relationship demonstrates a way of being with another person in which you experience feeling connected.

Are friendships relationships or recreationships? If you have a close friend with whom you share a natural affinity and experience a connection, then you have a relationship. You may recreate within the relationship, but a relationship has more depth to it than the recreationship.

In contrast to involvements and entanglements, a relationship seems easy because you come from sufficiency, adequacy, and abundance. You feel good about yourself.

Board of Directors

You base your present relationships on your training and conditioning. Your parents tend to be projections of your Board of Directors, of internal aspects existing within your personality. These aspects or tapes function as voices inside you that dictate your thinking, feeling, and behavior.

The Chairman of the Board is your aware self, who you is. The second member is yourself as a child. As a person, you were first a child. Depending on your training and conditioning, your child may be Adaptive or Rebellious or a combination of those traits. At any rate, the child member includes all the recordings of your experiences of you as a child.

The third member of your Board of Directors is your mother. With your mother, you formed the most profound, powerful life-forming relationship. And so it follows that your father is the fourth member. Even if your father wasn't present, your thoughts about him, your fantasies about being or not being like him, influenced your future. And Mom and Dad, as members of the Board of Directors, became your prototypes for future relationships.

How the Board Influences Your Relationships

So who do you think you marry first? Depending on whether you're male or female, you pick Mom or Dad. Let me illustrate the pattern from the male perspective.

The first time, you pick a sweet woman who fusses over you, tries to please you, takes care of you. And the marriage goes well for awhile; after all, she's just like your mother. Good old Mom. But soon, your wife seems childlike, innocent, even a little dumb. And she is so boring. Finally, you divorce her.

Next time, you may marry Mom again. But probably, you will pick someone with qualities like Dad. Let's say you meet someone at work, in a staff meeting. Now, this woman is really exciting; she has great ideas which she presents assertively; and she gets things done. You date her for awhile, and the relationship seems like a great adventure. Eventually, you marry her and your life seems colorful and exciting. But then, you discover this lady knows how to argue; in fact, she can talk circles around you. And she's too independent. And she doesn't take care of you or the house. Better divorce her.

Who do you marry next? Some men marry the Child Board Member. You see that in May/December marriages. Through the person who exhibits a strong free child, you can access your own natural child. You can experience your emotions directly and have a great time.

So the three characters on your Board of Directors—Mother, Father, Child— provide you with the checklist you use to select your relationship partners. You choose the option that best fits the pattern of your training and conditioning. And sometimes you choose a

---

Oh my God, I married my mother

P: If you realize you married your mother, what can you do to save your relationship?

Tony: Recognizing that you originally based your relationship on the form of your mother can be a starting point for increased awareness, understanding, and acceptance in the relationship. You don't have to go to divorce court. Just use the information to look beyond your projection to the loving human being behind it.

P: My husband and I both married our mother. And we use the awareness to laugh about our relationship. One of us may say, "Now, Mom, cut it out," or "Okay Mom, . . ."

Tony: That's great. Your awareness coupled with humor can be a great tool for enlightenment and for lightening up the seriousness we impose on our relationships. Humor can catapult you out of your training and conditioning.

composite personality, for example, one that includes characteristics of both Mom and Dad.

Eventually, you tire of the form, which usually begins to disintegrate when the games surface. The partner no longer measures up to the paragon you call Mom or Dad.

Sometimes people come from homes in which their parents' marriage seems fine. So as adults, they pick a partner who will fit that pattern. On the surface, the relationship seems okay, but when serious problems erupt, the relationship falls apart because the person lacks a model for handling relationship problems. Their parents had problems, too, but they hid them. In a real relationship, you will travel into territory with no guideposts, so you have to function free-form. You have to rely on your aware self—use purpose as a guide.

Be Aware of Your Training and Conditioning

It's important to be aware of your personal training and conditioning patterns, as well as what you specifically project about your parents onto your relationships. The following process should clarify some of your basic relationship problems.

That's not me, or is it?

P: What if a trait is exactly opposite from the way you are?

Tony: That's a sure sign that you've got it. The characteristic belongs to you. You focus your awareness on being the opposite of the item on your list, and then whatever you resist persists in you. You use your act to cover up the trait from others as well as from yourself. What is the trait?

P: I remember it bugged me when my mother was so busy, especially in clubs and social groups. And now, I stay away from things like that; I purposely avoid clubs.

Tony: What do you do instead?

P: Well, I stay pretty busy . . .

Tony: You're busy not being busy. You may not be busy attending club meetings, but you use something else to fill up your time. Either way, you're still busy.

Write down the three things about your same sex parent that you had the greatest trouble with as a child. Try to list personality qualities or characteristics. Don't list "my mother was an alcoholic"; instead, describe how she was when she drank. Which of her behaviors did you hate most? If you can't think of personality qualities, then list behaviors. Base the list on the first ten to twelve years of your life.

When you've finished, look at your list. First of all, the three things you listed describe the things you have the most trouble seeing about yourself, because you don't like them. You tend to deny them. Second, the list represents the aspects of your own personality with which you have the greatest trouble dealing. Third, the three characteristics cost you the most in your relationships and deplete your aliveness.

A Miracle

You can relate to others from three positions: your act, your game, or the self. If you operate from self, you know that inside every human being exists the potential for love and caring. You don't leave the relationship simply because you married your dad. You work with that in order to break out of the closed loop pattern. Awareness is not enough. Awareness, action, and a good dose of humor can break the loop.

A relationship is really a miracle. A miracle expands you, permits you to realize your perfection and wholeness. The miracle of relationship is obtainable, not through seeking forms or projections of your parents, but through recognition of and willingness to see and to include others in the universe of the Aware and Related Self.

Love and Loving

If I love you,
I unconditionally accept you
If I am loving with you,
I share myself with you
If you love me,
you will unconditionally accept me
If you are loving with me,
you share yourself with me
I want you to know
I love you loving me
and I know
You love me loving you

The Care and Feeding of Good Relationships

Guided Fantasy

Close your eyes now. Breathe deeply and fully. Allow yourself to relax completely and slowly go into your center. Focus on your mantra if you like or allow yourself to move into a meditative state.

Good. And now, think about someone you are in a relationship with. Go back in time with that person. Go back to the point at which you remember your first true communication. Go beyond a simple exchange of information. Instead, experience a level of connectedness that transcended ordinary, daily communication. Notice your interaction with this person and observe the dynamics of true communication.

Fine. And let the scene go. Now think of a time in the relationship in which you discussed your purpose and goals with your partner. Can you remember a time when you and your partner talked about your reason for being in the relationship? Notice if you actually discussed purpose or if you discussed what form the relationship would take. Did you consider that person to be a vehicle for acquiring certain forms in your life, or did you see the relationship as a foundation for feeling generally loving, capable, and connected?

Good. And let that scene go. And now remember the games you

played or still play with each other. Recall a time when you argued, attacked, or withdrew from each other. Look at your partner's reaction and try to determine what his or her negative ground-of-being might be. And then, consider your own games and how you use them to hide the negative beliefs and feelings you have about yourself.

Finally, return to your position of observer. And consider what you would like for your partner to do so that you could grow and move forward on your path. How can your partner support your purpose and the purpose of the relationship?

Now, take a moment to distance yourself from your partner. Take time to explore further the other person's reality. What does this person like? What does he want? What does he dislike? And then, allow yourself to move into a heightened awareness about your partner. And from a position of enlightenment, know and understand what you can do to support your partner in his own growth, based on his own needs. See clearly how you can feed your partner's river.

Let all the images go. Return slowly to the present, to this room, bringing with you new awareness about yourself and your relationships.

The Five Processes

How do you avoid entanglements and involvements? How can you transform an involvement into a relationship?

To create and maintain a relationship, you need to complete five processes:

- ◆ Explore each other's reality.
- ◆ Create a purpose.
- ◆ Establish a form.
- ◆ Set up strategies for handling the craziness.
- ◆ Feed each other's river.

Exploring Each Other's Reality

In the first process—exploring each other's reality—you expand your sense of self to include the other person. The expansion occurs within the extraordinary universe and depends on your ability to communicate intimately with each other. So, what is communication? The dictionary defines it as "the exchange of information." Within the ordinary universe, communication includes sharing, sending, and receiving messages.

How You Communicate: Three Levels

That kind of everyday communication is essential to a relationship. However, in the extraordinary universe, Werner Erhard defines communication as "the intentional and harmonious recreation of another person's experience." Extraordinary communication in a relationship means you explore the unique reality and experience of another person in addition to your own. You possess a cosmic awareness through which you feel the entire universe.

Level A: Your Act

Most of us, however, communicate from our positions in the ordinary universe. At the beginning of a relationship, we usually interact superficially: "Pretty weather we're having today," you might say. And your friend responds, "Sure is. Hope it stays that way." Those two people aren't communicating with each other; they are conversing through their acts. Your act is the socially acceptable facade or persona you present to most of the world. It is you at your best, with best being defined by your training and conditioning.

Level B: Your Game

The second level of communication surfaces in a relationship soon after the act wears thin. At the game level, you set up patterns of behavior and communication which guarantee negative feelings. Actually, you feel badly—angry, hurt, scared—before your interaction, but you blame the feeling on someone else. You use games to discredit your partner while you elevate yourself.

When you communicate out of your act or game, you condemn your relationship to a stagnant existence in the ordinary universe. Your act and your game originate in your mind; they are part of what you are, but they are not who you is.

Level C: Your Self

True, effortless communication is possible, but only in the extraordinary universe. It emanates, not from the mind, but from the self. In a real relationship, exploring each other's reality means going beyond your partner's act and game and moving toward discovery of who he/she is.

What You Communicate: Three Levels

While it's important to notice *how* you communicate, it's equally important to notice *what* you communicate. Are you communicating out of content, feeling, or context?

◆ **Content.** At the content level, communication consists of what is verbalized. About thirty-five percent of our communication with others occur at the content level.

◆ **Feeling.** At the feeling level, you communicate on the basis of your needs and projections. Feelings, including your negative ground-of-being, motivate your conversation. And you form the content, whatever you verbalize, to fit your needs.

◆ **Context.** At the level of context, you communicate from your aware self—consciously and intentionally. A relationship based on communication out of self and context becomes effortless and connected. It exists only in the extraordinary universe and requires unconditional acceptance of self and others.

Creating a Purpose

Once you've established a context, you move toward the second requirement for a successful relationship—creating a purpose. The purpose must come from your awareness and choice about how you want to experience yourself. Through your purpose, you decide what you want to accomplish in the relationship; you decide on the desired outcome.

Without a purpose, your relationship lacks direction and may even move backward. A relationship is a process, not a frozen entity. Because your environment and life circumstances change, the form of your

> ## Communication in a marital relationship
>
> **P:** What about a marital relationship? Even when you come from self, don't you still need to communicate at the content level?
>
> **Tony:** Marriage can be viewed as either content or context. Most people approach marriage only at the content level. They base their form of marriage, what they think it should be and want it to be, on their training and conditioning, which is usually negative, or at least limiting.
>
> On the other hand, marriage as context, as a framework for mutually agreeable content, is an opportunity or a space for two people to grow, to move, to support each other.

relationship changes by necessity. So, you must commit to the purpose, not to the form of the relationship.

Most relationships originate in a short-term commitment to form: dinner together, a good time, some companionship. Partners explore each other's reality from a comfortable distance. But soon, you come to a choice point at which you decide to end the relationship, or to escalate it. If you decide to continue the relationship, this is the time to discuss your purpose, to communicate further to be sure you're talking about purpose and not about form.

Your Purpose as a Guiding Star

In any relationship, use your purpose as a guiding star. Your purpose includes whatever you want to generate, create, or manifest in your relationship with another human being.

Ultimately, you're in a relationship to be related. Use your communication skills to find out what the other person wants specifically. And listen to your own heart to determine what you want.

What if the purpose is different in a relationship? For instance, you may want to feel loved and loving, while your partner may want to feel capable. Are your purposes compatible? Yes. You just need to create forms or agreements within the relationship so that both purposes are fulfilled. You don't have to have the same purpose to support the other person or to be supported yourself.

Remember a purpose is general, directional, positive, and experiential. And remember too that you are your greatest source and resource. You are the true source of your experience of yourself as loving, loved, or capable. The other person or your partner simply enhances that experience. Through the relationship you both expand your universe to include the other.

Establishing a Form

You establish a form or structure for your purpose to make it more real and less theoretical. The third step needed to maintain a relationship involves the mechanics of the relationship. Unfortunately, we usually place the third step before the second step. The form actually should spring out of the purpose, not vice versa.

Based on the work you've already done in steps one and two, you place your purpose within a framework that both of you can live with and participate in. You build a mutually supportive structure on the foundation of your purpose.

For example, if you decide you want to experience yourself as warm and loving, playful and joyful, together you create agreements concerning who will do what to whom and when so that each of you feels loved, loving, and capable.

There is no limit to the forms into which you can mold your relationship. As you create your form, you explore your tapes and conditioning. It's important to check within to determine if the form you want is really what you want, as self, rather than as mind.

Let's say one of you wants to spend more time with the other. You both may agree to a form which calls for dinner together three times a week.

Or on the other hand, what if your partner wants some space, likes to be alone? You allow for that by providing him with the time to be alone—say, a couple of hours every day, or a whole weekend away once a month. Then, your relationship meets the needs of the couple as well as that of the individual.

The key to negotiation is diplomatic communication with each other. You don't demand a certain form; you suggest it, describe it, and then, negotiate the terms, within the context of your purpose.

How to Kill a Relationship

You can kill your relationship in any of three ways. Each behavior represents a form of lying which is based on your negative ground-of-being.

Lie

The first victim in the death of the relationship is always the truth. You can reduce a relationship to an entanglement in two ways: by not telling

---

Keep both your immediate and long-term purpose in mind

P: Doesn't your purpose sometimes backfire? That happened to me the other day at work. A group of guys were unloading a truck, but had the forklift going downhill. After struggling with it, they realized they couldn't move the load back uphill. They asked me, their supervisor, what they should do. So I said, "Unload the forklift, turn it around, and push it back uphill." After I said that, they became sullen and uncommunicative. What happened?

Tony: You assumed an "I'll show 'em" position, instead of cooperating in a joint effort or purpose. What was your purpose?

P: To get the forklift working so the truck could be unloaded.

Tony: What was the purpose of your interaction with them?

P: I'd like to think I genuinely tried to accomplish the job.

Tony: How did you want your workers to feel?

P: I didn't care how they felt at the time. I just wanted the job done so they could get onto other jobs.

Tony: You can get the job done in a variety of ways. If you had expanded your purpose to include their purpose—which also was to unload the truck—you might have found a different strategy, which included diplomacy and space for their feelings.

Clarity about your desired outcome is essential to a successful relationship. Always keep your eye on the immediate and long-term purpose of your interaction. In fact, the situation offered you an opportunity to solve a problem while simultaneously creating conditions for your workers to feel effective and competent. You did have a purpose but it was short-sighted; it didn't allow for the resources you needed to accomplish present and future tasks.

---

the truth or by not being able to handle hearing the truth. Many people use truth to justify dropping into their negative ground-of-being. But truth, as opposed to the simple facts, means you selectively share your experience. You don't tell all the facts, but you do share your experience of yourself, the other person, and the relationship.

Attack

You can kill a relationship through attacking and blaming. You can accuse, make the other person wrong. Or you can withdraw, detach from the other person through overeating, drugs, overworking.

Placate

Finally, you can placate or please your relationship to death. When you please someone without a genuine desire to support them, your relationship lacks integrity. And even though your placation may protect you from your partner's negative response, you also limit aliveness in the relationship and become resentful.

Handling the Craziness

Even with the best intentions, your negative ground-of-being, your games, will surface occasionally in a real relationship. Then, you need to move into step four, which calls for handling the craziness. You and your partner must create strategies, in advance, and use skills to handle the crazy times.

In a genuine relationship, you function as partners. A problem can't be stated simply as, "What will I do when I go crazy?" Instead, the problem becomes mutual: "What will we do when I go crazy?" You avoid games of guilt and blame and opt for strategies which support each other and your purpose.

What, exactly, is craziness? Craziness is doing something that produces pain for yourself or another person. When you drop into negative payoff games, you hurt yourself and set up conditions that guarantee the other person's pain. We are all human, and regardless of our level of awareness, we still retain years of training and conditioning which may surface. So, in step four, you allow for the unavoidable.

Here's an example. Suppose you need space, some time to yourself, and you make that need part of your form. But when you go off alone for a few hours, you come back to attacks and accusations. What do you do? You can handle this craziness by first exploring your partner's reality, by realizing that her attacks probably are based on her fear that you don't want to be with her. So, you need to listen to her, find out what's really bothering her.

One strategy then would be to reassure her that you do want to spend time with her. Don't assume a defensive position. Whenever the craziness occurs, you must handle what is primarily unconscious through communication, patience, and understanding.

How to Manage the Games

How do you disconnect from your game? How do you handle a game when it surfaces in a real relationship?

In a real relationship, you don't respond in typical game fashion. You return to your purpose. Ask yourself, "What is the purpose of this relationship? Why are we interacting right now? What do I want to

---

When the agreements become more important than the relationship

P: What happens though, when you start out with your agreements—to mow the grass once week, for instance—but then meeting the agreements becomes more important than just being together and doing little things for each other.

Tony: You must keep sight of your purpose and always place your purpose ahead of your structure. Without a purpose, you forget why you've chosen the form; the agreements become meaningless. Maintaining the form becomes a chore and buries instead of strengthens the love.

P: I know a couple who always claim they can't spend time together; they can't go out, because they don't have the money.

Tony: That's a game, probably used to avoid intimacy. You can take an hour and a few dollars and go get a hot dog. The purpose is that you want to spend time together; eating is the medium. If you believe you must eat in a gourmet restaurant in order to spend quality time together, then you're too attached to your form.

---

accomplish by interacting with you?" So when the other person plays a game, center yourself and decide on your desired outcome.

Calling off the Game

When you call off your side of the game, the other party ultimately must call off his or her side of the game. Of course, he may escalate the game for awhile in an attempt to entice you back into the old pattern. But eventually, he will stop. And then, you have a chance to build the relationship on new ground.

So, step one in game management is call off your side so that you feel better about yourself. Step two is check your purpose to determine why you're interacting. Finally, the third step is: Since you've handled yourself, your own machinery, you are now ready to handle your partner. Now, you ask yourself, "How do I handle myself so that I reinforce desirable behaviors and extinguish undesirable behaviors in my partner?"

Feeding Each Other's River

After you recognize your own game and take responsibility for your own needs and craziness, then you can assume the role of observer. You are free to move to the fifth process needed to create a successful relationship: feeding each other's river.

When you feed someone's river, you take the time to support the other person's reality. You already know what they like and don't like. In the final stage, you develop an awareness and understanding of what you can do to support that person in her growth on her path. You find ways to feed her river; you create positive payoff games in the relationship out of love and caring for your partner.

If she likes flowers, you send her flowers. If he loves the beach, you take a vacation at the beach. The gesture can be small or large, but it must be something you choose and create. And you do it out of love, not for manipulation. Out of your capacity for aliveness, you create mutually positive payoff games which fulfill the purpose of your relationship.

You begin by focusing on the other person. You decide what

behaviors you want your partner to increase, and then, you ask your partner, "What do I have to do for you to do X?" The behaviors you want to increase might include spending more time together, giving more verbal support, receiving more affection, playing more. And because you are feeding your partner's river by asking how you can support him in increasing the behaviors you desire, you have a better chance of getting what you want. You're no longer being defensive or taking your partner's undesirable behavior personally. So, feeding your partner's river automatically feeds your own.

Be sure to reinforce your partner's cooperation with compliments and acknowledgment. When he doesn't do what you want, develop alternate strategies ahead of time.

Sometimes the most supportive thing you can do for someone is to let them be, to give them the space to be miserable. Let's face it: You don't have a magic wand. Even if you did, if he wants to be unhappy, you can't change that.

Only he can change his mind. Most of us, though, use our partner's unhappiness and projection of that unhappiness onto us as justification for our own unhappiness and retaliation.

Playing the victim game

P: Recently, I realized I've been playing the victim game while my husband plays persecutor. My husband has some financial problems with a business partner, and he feels resentful and angry. He projects that onto me, and I take it. Many times, I've felt so angry about his attacks that I couldn't feel any love for him anymore. But lately, I've learned not to take his behavior personally. I've learned to see it as a projection of his pain and fear. And then, suddenly, the criticism began to decrease, so that now, it is only occasional.

Tony: So, you realized that your victim game, which kept you locked in your anger and defensiveness, actually buried your love.

P: Yes. I let my hatred of his criticism bury my love, but when I decided not to play victim anymore, the relationship shifted. I refuse to feel persecuted. I just laugh at the criticism. Now, I realize my purpose was to get back in touch with the love. And I'm enjoying the new situation.

Remember that you can relate to someone else from any of three levels: your act, your game, your self. You can transform the relationship at the third level where you be in love with the person. Regardless of whether your partner runs an act, plays a game, or comes from self, your reaction is still your choice.

In a relationship, the choice point comes whenever your partner tells you a piece of truth that is bigger than you can handle. Most of us drop into game and use the other person's behavior to excuse our own. You can dramatize the truth, or you can be bigger than it is.

In the past, some of you buried your love. In the extraordinary universe, you can revive your love. You can decide to tap your capacity to love and create what you want in spite of the circumstances. Within your aware self, you can generate enough acceptance and love to melt the barriers.

The Choice Is Yours

The care and feeding of a relationship is not an easy thing. Calling off the game reveals the emotions within that you want to avoid through game playing. So, you have to be ready for the emotion to surface, and then allow yourself to experience it, to be bigger than it is.

Most of us would be happy if we could handle a relationship with just one person. Actually, you can create a relationship with the most unaware person in the world. In the extraordinary universe, you can experience a cosmic consciousness in which you feel connected to everything in the universe. It's simply and fully a matter of choice.

Fear of Loving You/Me

My fear of loving you
is directly related to
my fear of loving me
My capacity to love you
is directly related to
my capacity to love me
My willingness to love you
is directly related to
my willingness to love me
I am willing to love you
I am willing to love me

Completion: Laying the Groundwork for Future Relationships

Guided Fantasy

Close your eyes and take a few deep breaths. Allow yourself to relax. Clear your mind, letting go of any concerns or anxieties you've held onto during the day. And now, do a body scan, starting with your feet. Notice any tense areas; breathe into those areas, relaxing them. Move up through your body, identifying and releasing tight areas until you feel completely relaxed. Begin to center yourself, gradually moving into your safe space, and meditate, using your mantra.

Now, see yourself walking in your safe space. And as you walk, you become younger and younger. Look ahead of you now and see your father step out of a wooded area. He stands before you, and you greet him.

Take this opportunity to share with him what you learned from him about relationships. Tell him how you decided to protect yourself, to express love, to handle conflict. Tell him how you feel about your relationship with him and what you've taken into future relationships as a result. Tell him your truth. Take some time now to let him know that you're willing to let him succeed as your father. Tell him you know that he did everything he could do, knew how to do, as your father. Is there anything you need to forgive him for or ask his forgiveness for? Do that now. When you're ready, thank him for coming and tell him good-bye.

Continue up the mountain, climbing higher and getting younger. The path levels off once again and you see a clearing ahead. Your mother steps out into the clearing. Notice the expression on her face, in her eyes. Let her see you, too. Share with her now what you learned from her. What did she teach you about relationships?

Is there anything you need to forgive her for? Forgiveness means you give up your need to punish or be angry. It means letting go of your position that she wasn't quite good enough as your mother. Let her know she made it as your mother. When you've shared your truth, thank her for coming and let her go.

Continue up the mountain, going higher and higher, becoming still younger. You arrive at another level area which looks out over the entire valley. Out of the woods walks someone with whom you were very close at one time. You really loved this person, and you knew he really loved you. Watch the person approach you now and share a hug.

Take your loved one by the hand, and walk over to a ledge where you sit down. Let your feet dangle over the edge and, together, look out over the valley. Sit quietly, holding hands, and then share with this individual what your relationship with him meant to you and what you learned from it.

When you are ready, say good-bye to your friend. Begin to return to the present, bringing with you a new awareness about your relationship with your parents. Open your eyes and look directly in to the eyes of your partner.

One of you should begin first, finishing the sentence: "I am a person who . . ." Repeat the sentence, allowing yourself to create new endings. Don't censor yourself; be with whatever words come up for you. And then, allow your partner to complete the same sentence stem. Repeat the process, looking into each other's eyes, one of you listening while the other speaks.

Now, imagine that the person in front of you is your mother. Take a deep breath and get in touch with past and present feelings about your mother. And then, speak to your partner as if he were your mother. Complete the sentence fragments below, repeating each phrase several times.

"What I appreciate about you most is . . ."

"What scares or threatens me in our relationship is . . ."

"What I need and want from you is . . ."

When one person has completed all three sentences, the other person should begin the process, projecting his mother's image onto the partner.

Then, repeat the exercise, but this time project your father's image onto your partner's face. When both of you have finished completing the sentence, take time to share your experience.

Completing Parental Relationships

Many of us have never handled our relationships with our parents. We have not allowed our connection to them to be complete and whole. Consequently, we bring the resentments, and the incompletions with Mom and Dad, into present and future relationships. We project the content of growing up in the past onto the potential aliveness of the present and future.

To complete your relationship with your parents, you must create a context that originates in who you is, in the extraordinary universe of creation and choice.

In completing your relationship with your parents, you neither add to it nor take away from it. You allow the relationship to be okay the way it is. That doesn't mean you eliminate the issues or problems. You will still feel angry, hurt, and resentful occasionally, but you realize the issues and feelings are content, not context. When you complete the relationship based on context, you expand your sense of self to include and allow for the problems.

The Forgiveness Process

Part of the completion process is forgiveness. In the guided fantasy, we defined forgiveness as the willingness to give up the need to punish the other person. In the forgiveness process, you voluntarily relinquish your anger about your parents' mistakes.

If you allow for and create a context which involves acceptance and forgiveness, then even the negative content becomes evidence that you do love them. You create a space within and surrender your resistance to and struggle with the content.

Content

Content includes your tapes, all the unexperienced experiences, all the negative feelings you hang onto. You use the content to project the blame for your unhappiness onto your parents.

Actually, you are the author of your misery. Long ago, you created the content, which makes you the source of your continuing negative experience with your parents.

Forgiving a father

P: I can forgive my dad for what he did and didn't do for me when I was little. But now, his drinking problem comes between us. I could complete the relationship in terms of the past, except for his refusal to own his alcoholism.

Tony: Then you're not ready to forgive and allow your father to succeed as your dad. As long as you focus on the content of your father's drinking problem, and until you accept him as he is, you will create ripples in your other relationships. It's okay to want him to get better, but you can't use the condition of his getting better as context.

P: Then, my relationship with him is incomplete because I'm imposing a condition on it. But all I want now is to sit down and talk to him. I feel our relationship won't be complete until we can do that. And I feel we can't do that because he won't admit he drinks too much.

Tony: Talking is content. You're hooking onto a function of the ordinary universe, a condition which you are unwilling to release. As long as you refuse to accept him unconditionally as your parent, you will continue to dramatize and play out the incompletion in future relationships.

Many of us made decisions about our parents when we were very young. We decided, out of our disillusionment and anger, that our parents weren't going to make it with us. If only they'd done it right— "if only they'd loved me more, bought me more, taken me to more places—then, my life would have been better than it is now."

That's your content. It's also your position, and it keeps you from completing your relationship with them. Surrendering your position, looking at context instead of content, requires some ego destruction. And at first, the process may seem contradictory and confusing.

You will have to interpret the fact that your father left and your mother never told you she loved you as evidence that they did in fact love you. In the past, you've taken the negative circumstances as evidence for the content, which left you feeling rejected. Now, you must use the circumstances as evidence for the context. And since context cannot be negative, then all negative circumstances must be viewed as positive proof of your parents' love for you.

Context

You create a context in the extraordinary universe. "Dad never loved me" is the content of the ordinary universe. The content is not real; it is only your arbitrary interpretation of events and circumstances.

Only the context is real. After all, you had your first experience of aliveness, of being related and connected, through your relationship with your parents. But over the years, you covered up the context with content. Out of your fear of rejection and abandonment, you lose sight of the contextual love already present and available to you.

Because you've buried your early experience of fundamental love, you believe you can't recreate it in your present relationships. And the negative feelings remain locked within you, because you've refused to experience them. By hanging on to the content, by refusing to experience it out, you preclude the possibility of experiencing the context.

Completion Is Essential to Future Relationships

How do you complete the relationship with your parents? First, be aware of your position. How do you feel about the relationship? What do you need to do to complete it? How can you allow them to succeed as your parents?

Second, continue the forgiveness process you began in the guided fantasy. What do you need to forgive them for? What content do you need to let go of? Be certain as you do the forgiveness process that you are sincere and truly willing to release your unexperienced feelings

---

You never talk to me anymore

P: My wife and I had an argument last night, and all the old barriers went up again. She wanted to talk, when I wanted to sleep. It was 12:30 A.M., and I had to get up in six hours.

Tony: So that was the trigger.

P: Yes. She's very insecure and needs me to tell her how I feel all the time. In my family, we didn't talk about feelings. I knew I had them, but I kept them to myself. And now, sometimes I don't even know what they are, so how can I share them? I have given more compliments and paid more attention to her lately, but it's still not enough.

Really, her comment that we were drifting apart, that we weren't close, triggered me. I agree we weren't close last week because she was out of town all week. The day she returned, she expected me to drop plans I made three weeks ago, just because she came home. Anyway, she kept talking while I tried to sleep. Finally, I kicked into my game and we had a fight.

Tony: You're most vulnerable to your game when you're tired and stressed. It's hard to come from center during those times. Nevertheless, how could you have handled it differently?

P: I could have ignored the conversation and said I wouldn't talk about it until morning when I could respond better. But then, she'd accuse me of avoiding the issue.

Tony: You could tell her you understand how she feels and you'd like to talk about it more so it won't happen again. And then ask if you could talk about it at lunchtime tomorrow when you can think more clearly?

P: She'd probably accept that.

Tony: Sounds like you both have issues around rejection and control. And where did those feelings and issues originate? With your parents.

---

about the relationship. And then, realize that your parents did a pretty good job. After all, you've made it this far in life; they must have taught you enough to lead to some success in your life.

Broken Stove Syndrome

As adults, we work diligently to repair present relationships, but it's the past that needs fixing. Our dilemma resembles the problem of the man with the broken stove. The man goes after his tool kit and busily proceeds to work on the refrigerator. In fact, he spends hours working on the refrigerator. Finally, he walks over and turns on the stove, and the darn thing still doesn't work! That's how most of us work on our relationships. Our refusal to complete the relationship with our parents alters other significant relationships.

Giving Up Resistance

Going through the forgiveness process with your parents can decrease the size of your negative ground and reduce the energy you spend on resistance games with them and others. In this process, you must be big enough to leave behind your resistance. Move toward creating a context of acceptance. Allow your partner to be himself; accept what he does instead of using it to trigger your game. If you do hook into it, let the tapes play, but don't believe them. Be an observer, instead.

Each time you don't play the game, the resistance weakens. Eventually, you create the relationship as complete, regardless of what it consists of and in spite of what your partner does or doesn't do.

When you can do that with your parents, you might finally realize that your parents have always had total, absolute love for you. The only thing that has limited that love has been their inability to express it the way you wanted it.

The creation of a context occurs outside of time, which means it can happen instantly. You don't need to wait until you've accumulated all the evidence that it's okay to complete your relationship. You don't have to wait until your father's stopped drinking or your mother's stopped criticizing you or they've both stopped dominating you. The content will never be exactly right.

So, you might as well go on and create the context from which you can love them regardless of the content. You can create the context to include the drinking, the criticizing, the domination, as a part rather than the whole of the relationship.

You have the power to create a context by your consideration alone. Your willingness to complete the relationship can make it happen.

"I Forgive You"

You don't necessarily have to say aloud that you forgive your parents to complete your relationship with them. You can change a behavior or end a game.

For example, I knew a man who resisted his mother's domination through withholding. He shared that his mother wanted him to be happy and feel good about himself. So, every time he went home, he would deny his own well-being. He told her how unhappy he was and how badly his life had turned out.

Most of us find out what others want from us, and then withhold ourselves as a way to punish them. It's a technique for avenging old insults and injuries.

Allow Your Parents to "Make It" as Parents

To complete the relationship, you give up your desire for revenge, and instead, communicate with your parents so that they know they've succeeded as your parents. After all, you made it; you survived. Since your survival was their responsibility, they did succeed at a fundamental level. And not only did you grow up and survive, but you accomplished a few things as well.

So what are you so mad at them about? Why do you withhold your acceptance and your love from them?

Give them a break. Go up to your mother or father or both and tell them they did their job. Tell them they were successful and that you recognize and love them for a job well done.

Now, your parents may or may not be in a space to hear you, to respond gracefully to you. If they are, that's great. If they're not, then stay centered, and continue the forgiveness process. Some of us make our parents wrong, because they're not in our space. And then, we use our awareness as a way to be right.

Don't use your awareness as a weapon to make your parents understand you. You must understand them. Love them by being big enough to handle their craziness, regardless of how they respond to you. Use your awareness to strengthen and move you toward mastery.

Out of your mastery and awareness, you accept yourself as loving, complete, and whole. From that space, you perceive your parents as whole and loving, and you choose to relate to that part of them. Once you've established a context with your parents, you have a greater chance of approaching your other relationships from acceptance and eventually mastery.

Context Includes the Negative

To create a context out of the extraordinary universe, you have to admit that both of you and your partner have your own craziness. A context includes all the negatives; you acknowledge that the negative is present, but you don't buy into it. You don't use it to arouse your negative ground-of-being or to play games.

Just as you both have craziness, you both have love. Your context is that you love your partner, and that any interaction with him becomes evidence of the love.

Strategies: Place vs. Space

She wants to talk to him, but he doesn't want to talk. The context includes her need to talk to him, as well as his reluctance to talk. What strategy should she use?

If her purpose is to share her feelings with him, then she can approach him from place or space. In the ordinary universe, she would resist his lack of response and fall into her negative ground-of-being. He's not about to listen to her when she fights him, and her outcome will be the opposite of what she wants. Actually, she's coming from a place, a position, rather than from a space.

On the other hand, she can approach him from a space of loving, sharing, and feeling. She can accept the relationship as it is, while recognizing there's room for improvement. Out of that space, she creates strategies for getting what she wants from him. But she pursues it with detachment. If she tries strategy A to get him to listen and it doesn't work, then she tries plan B. If that worked better, but B is still not right, she tries C. It works, and he listens to her 50 percent of the time, which is an improvement. The process then becomes a dance instead of a win-lose game.

Part of the dance, for example, might be that she wait until it's a good time to talk. She watches and notices when he might be more receptive. That's strategy.

What if she tries all the strategies and he still doesn't want to listen?

Acceptance vs. submission

P: My husband tends to ignore me too, and I'm still not sure what to do. Lately, I've been saying to my husband, "I want you to listen to me and acknowledge what I'm saying and show some empathy. I want to explain why I'm upset, or nervous." But that's not accepting him, is it? If I truly accepted him, then I would accept his ignoring me.

Tony: No, you're talking about submission; I'm talking about acceptance. Submission implies that you lie down on the floor with "Walk on Me" stencilled on your shirt. Acceptance means you stop resisting his behavior.

You decide it's okay if he attempts to dominate you, and you give up any resistance to being dominated by him. That doesn't mean you move yourself into a position where you let him dominate you. Simply give up your resistance to his attempt, his need to dominate you. Say to yourself, "He needs to feel powerful and he tries to dominate me so he can feel good. That's where he is, that's what he does, and that's okay."

Once you stop resisting, you are free to do other things. You can consciously choose your response and search for alternatives to handling his need to dominate. You don't submit to the way he is, but you do acknowledge it. Then, instead of trying to change him, you find creative ways to live with him with integrity. Otherwise, you become locked into your resistance as much as he is locked into his domination. The more you resist him controlling you, the more you're controlled by him.

If he doesn't want to listen to her, she still doesn't have to submit to his domination. At that point, she might check her purpose and decide whether she wants to stay in an entanglement or not.

Otherwise, she should work toward creating the things she wants to happen in the relationship, but do it from a position of play. She should do it from a position of joy and fun, exploring and love. She should create a context in which she knows the relationship is perfect just the way it is. And that both of she and her partner are perfect as they are.

More on Strategies

Let's say your mother has dominated you for years. Every time you're around her, she nags you. And ever since you were a kid, you've resisted her domination. So, give up your resistance to being dominated by her. Let her do whatever she's doing and allow the relationship to be complete and whole as it is, and then decide what you're going to do next.

In the creation of a context, nothing is implied as to what you should or shouldn't do. You create the context so that you can experience yourself and your relationship as joyful, loving, and complete.

At some point though, you may decide there's not enough joy or play in the relationship, so you give it a new form. You decide to cut your visits to your mother from every weekend to only the holidays.

As always, you have a choice. Your happiness depends simply on your willingness to consider yourself happy. And in the context of that happiness, you get sad and angry sometimes; occasionally, you feel rejected, hurt, and depressed. Nevertheless, you accept and create your life as happy and joyful in the context of love.

The essence of completion depends on your power, your ability to transcend the games. You create a context which allows the relationship to be perfect—so perfect that it includes, even embraces, all the imperfections. If you can do that with your parents, then you can do it with anybody.

Freedom

In the depths of thought we always lose
The things we seek to find
In the search for love we always choose
The things that please our mind

But mind and heart too often see
They cannot bond as one
And mind through logic seeks to be
The ruler of the sun

We seek the path we truly feel
Will lead us to be free
But in the end, when all is still
An empty world we see

For in the end it is not thought
That brings our fear's release
It's love that stops the wars we've fought
And brings us final peace

So stop the battles—end the wars
Return again to love
Take down the cage—remove the bars
The eagle turns to dove

Tom Caperton

Conclusion:
Playing the Game of Life

What would a life of love and laughter be like? Simply, you would experience the whole of life available to you in both the extraordinary and ordinary universes. You would know that your life—all of it—was perfect and complete, right now. In short, you would clearly and happily be.

Your life, then, would become a game you played in order to have particular experiences. But, your game would have primarily positive rather than negative payoffs. And, as in any game, you would follow the rules required to win.

What are the rules of enlightened living? First, don't get too attached to the process. After all, your life is a game which you create.

Second, living masterfully requires that you give up what you are attached to. At the same time, let go of the past. Once you've stopped living in the past and dreaming about the future, you can focus on what keeps you on, or off purpose.

Now that you're clear about the basic rules of the game, what moves lead to mastering the game of life?

◆ Whenever you encounter a barrier, return to square one—your purpose. Then, keep moving by expanding your purpose to include the barrier. Let it be part of your purpose.

◆ If you find yourself off purpose, examine it to see if you chose the wrong purpose. Be willing to give up failed purposes and do it with integrity. As a master of your life, not only do you accept responsibility for the mess you've created, but you also clean it up.

◆ Don't stop your forward motion to handle the mess. Create a new purpose that genuinely meets the needs of who you are right now. Consider, out of your joy and aliveness, what you want. Then, explore what you need to do to become a master of living, loving, and laughing in your own universe.

When you've figured that out, when you think you've found the ideal purpose, goal, and strategy, give up your struggle. Relax in the extraordinary awareness that you and your life are already perfect.

And then, do it. Live out of your awareness. Use what you are—your mind, body, and emotions—to express and celebrate who you is: always in process—the perfect self.

Suggested Reading For Personal Awareness

Babcock & Keepers, *Raising Kids OK*

Bach, Richard, *Jonathan Livingston Seagull, Illusions*

Berne, Eric, *What Do You Say After You Say Hello?, Games People Play*

Brandon, Nathaniel, *The Disowned Self*

Castaneda, Carlos, *The Teachings of Don Juan, A Separate Reality, Journey to Ixtlan, Tales of Power, The Second Ring of Power, The Eagle's Gift*

Emery, Stewart, *Actualizations*

Ferguson, Marilyn, *The Aquarian Conspiracy*

Frederick, Carl, *EST, (Playing the Game the New Way)*

Harris, Thomas A., *I'm OK— You're OK*

Heinlein, Robert A., *Stranger in a Strange Land, Time Enough for Love*

James & Jongeward, *Born to Win*

Jongeward & Scott, *Women as Winners*

Paul, Margaret & Jordan, *Do I Have to Give Up Me to be Loved by You?*

Keirsey & Bates, *Please Understand Me*

Kopp, Sheldon, *If You Meet the Buddha on the Road, Kill Him*

Le Shan, *How to Meditate*

Lilly, John C., *Simulations of God, The Dyadic Cyclone, The Center of the Cyclone*

Lowen, Alexander, *Bioenergetics*

Meininger, Jut, *Success Through Transactional Analysis*

Naisbitt, John, *Megatrends*

Pearce, Joseph Chilton, *Exploring the Crack in the Cosmic Egg*

Perls, Frederick S., *In and Out the Garbage Pail*

Rajneesh, Bhagwan Shree, *Mustard Seed*

Satir, Virginia, *Peoplemaking*

Shapiro, Deane H., Jr., *Precision Nirvana*

Shutz, Will, *Joy, Profound Simplicity*

Steiner, Claude, *Scripts People Live*

Index